THE IRISH-AMERICANS

This is a volume in the Arno Press collection

THE IRISH-AMERICANS

Advisory Editor
Lawrence J. McCaffrey

Editorial Board
Margaret E. Conners
David N. Doyle
James P. Walsh

*See last pages of this volume
for a complete list of titles*

THE MAKING OF AN IMMIGRANT CITY

Ethnic and Cultural Conflict
in Jersey City, New Jersey
1850-1877

Douglas V. Shaw

ARNO PRESS
A New York Times Company
New York — 1976

F
144
.J5
S46
1976

Editorial Supervision: ANDREA HICKS

———◆———

First publication in book form, 1976,
  by Arno Press, Inc.
Copyright © 1973 by Douglas V. Shaw

THE IRISH-AMERICANS
ISBN for complete set: 0-405-09317-9
See last pages of this volume for titles.

Manufactured in the United States of America

———◆———

Library of Congress Cataloging in Publication Data

Shaw, Douglas V
    The Making of an immigrant city.

    (The Irish-Americans)
    Originally presented as the author's thesis, University of Rochester, 1972.
    1. Irish Americans--New Jersey--Jersey City--Politics and government. 2. Jersey City--Politics and government. 3. Nativism. I. Title. II. Series.
F144.J5S46 1976   301.45'19'162074926   76-6366
ISBN 0-405-09358-6

THE MAKING OF AN IMMIGRANT CITY:
ETHNIC AND CULTURAL CONFLICT
IN JERSEY CITY, NEW JERSEY,
1850-1877

by

Douglas V. Shaw

Submitted in Partial Fulfillment
of the
Requirements for the Degree

DOCTOR OF PHILOSOPHY

Supervised by   Professor Herbert G. Gutman
Department of   History

The University of Rochester
Rochester, New York
1972

For Virginia

ACKNOWLEDGEMENTS

Although a thesis has but one author, it is in many ways a cooperative endeavor. I am especially indebted to Professor Herbert G. Gutman, who directed the work, and Professor Ronald P. Formisano, who also carefully read and criticized the manuscript. Both worked diligently to keep my wandering thoughts in some sort of order. To Professor Gutman goes my additional gratitude for consistent enthusiasm, honest and constructive criticism in matters of style and emphasis, invaluable aid in interpreting the data in Chapter II, and, of course, the idea itself.

Others helped facilitate the research process. Invariably the personnel of the libraries I used were cooperative and friendly. The staff of the Jersey City Public Library went out of their way to provide me with the necessary materials, both in the library and through inter-library loan. I owe a special note of thanks to the library's Archivist, J. Owen Grundy, whose knowledge of Jersey City history and of the local sources was of great value. The inter-library loan department of the University of Rochester's library exerted itself to track down materials that were obscure and difficult to obtain. The staffs of New York Public Library, the New Jersey State Library in Trenton, and the New Jersey Historical

Society in Newark also provided necessary assistance in pleasant surroundings.

Five people read and criticized the manuscript in various stages of its development. Professors Gutman and Formisano followed it from beginning to end. Peter Herman and Ann Smythers read substantial portions and offered me sound advice. My wife, Virginia, not only read and corrected it, forcing clarity in ideas and wording, but drew the maps and typed the final copy.

My intellectual debt to Professor Gutman is great. Those who know his work will see his influence throughout the dissertation. He has been a firm, but fair, critic.

The New Jersey Historical Commission provided a grant-in-aid that helped to underwrite my research expenses.

PREFACE

In 1850 Jersey City, a residential suburb of New York City, was governed by native-born Protestant members of the city's economic elite. By 1880 it had become an urban center of transportation and industry, governed largely by Irish Catholics of working class and lower middle class background. This important political transition followed changes in the city's population from native-born to immigrant, from Protestant to Catholic, from predominantly middle and upper class to largely working and lower middle class. Although the population had changed most radically in the 1850's, the shift in political power occurred two decades later--during the 1870's. For a quarter of a century native-born Protestants resisted immigrant penetration of the city's institutions and through a variety of devices succeeded in delaying what had appeared inevitable.

In order to establish the relationship between economic class and ethnicity, I analyzed the 1860 Jersey City manuscript census, with particular emphasis on the city's native born and Irish populations, each about forty percent of the city. Relying largely on occupational data, I found, for example, that while only nine percent of the native-born males were unskilled laborers, over half of the Irish were unskilled. Correspondingly, the city's elite was overwhelmingly native-born. British and German immigrants, each about ten percent of the population, clustered in the skilled trades.

Jersey City's native-born population worked diligently to change Irish identity. Through the 1850's they gave heavy support to such organizations as the City Mission and Tract Society and the Hudson County Bible Society. Know-Nothingism had strong appeal, and the management of schools, jails, and the poor house reflected widespread anti-Catholic sentiment. These efforts to force cultural changes--termed moral reforms by the participants--failed. Resistance, continued immigration, and poverty left the Irish community as distinct in 1860 as it had been in 1850. In the meantime, however, the Irish began to gain political recognition. During the decade of the 1860's the Irish attained elective office, first as the pliant agents of native-born politicians and then in more independent and aggressive ways. These small successes, not surprisingly, nurtured the anti-Catholicism and nativism of the native-born community, convincing successive state legislatures to make many local offices nonelective. After Jersey City voters elected nearly all immigrants as city officials in 1870, fearful native-born citizens, Republicans and Democrats alike, created a city charter that turned the powers of local government over to commissioners appointed by the state legislature. In many ways the high tide of nativism in Jersey City, commission government lasted for six years, from 1871 to 1877. Only after the appointed commissions were repealed in 1877 did Jersey City's Catholic immigrant population attain the political power that their numbers in the city had so long warranted.

Most importantly, nativism and anti-Catholicism continued through and after the Civil War. In Jersey City and elsewhere, attempts to limit the political influence of Irish Catholics did not cease with the advent of war. By ignoring the war as an issue, this thesis traces the continuities of ethnic, class, and religious conflicts from the 1850's to the 1870's.

TABLE OF CONTENTS

	PAGE
Acknowledgements	iv
Preface	vi
List of Tables	x
List of Maps	xii

CHAPTERS

I	Introduction	1
II	The 1860 Jersey City Census	14
III	The Protestant City: Aspects of Nativism, 1850-1859	48
IV	Police, Courts, and the Irish, 1860-1868	90
V	The Transition to an Immigrant City, 1868-1870	135
VI	The Lace Curtain Revolt	168
VII	Nativism and the 1871 Commission Charter	199
VIII	Trials and Errors	235

A Note on Sources	266
Bibliography	269

LIST OF TABLES

TABLE		PAGE
I	All White Males Twenty and Older by Ethnicity, Jersey City, 1860..............	18
II	Occupations by Nativity, All Jersey City Males Twenty and Older, 1860........	21
III	Selected Jersey City Occupations by Ethnicity, White Males Twenty and Older, 1860............................	22
IV	Ethnicity by Selected Occupations, White Males Twenty and Older, Jersey City, 1860........................	27
V	Real Property Owned by Native-born and Irish, Fourth Ward, Jersey City, 1860...................................	28
VI	Occupations of Negro Males, Twenty and Older, Jersey City, 1860.................	29
VII	Size of Industrial Units by Number of Workers, Jersey City, 1860...............	30
VIII	Ethnicity of Selected Occupations, Jersey City, 1860.......................	32
IX	Occupation by Ethnicity, Males Fifteen to Nineteen, Jersey City, 1860...........	34
X	Native-born and Irish Women by Role and Age, Fourth Ward, Jersey City, 1860...................................	37
XI	Heads of Households by Sex, Fourth Ward, Jersey City, 1860..................	39
XII	Occupations of White Women, Fifteen and Older, Jersey City, 1860.............	40
XIII	Servants by Ethnicity and Age, Jersey City, 1860.............................	41
XIV	Servants and Employers by Ethnicity, Jersey City, 1860.......................	42

XV	Religious Affiliation by Family, Jersey City, 1856, 1865, 1869....................	44
XVI	Religious Affiliation by Family, Jersey City Germans, 1856, 1865.................	45
XVII	Comparison by Occupation of Know-Nothings, 1856, with All Native-born Males, Twenty and Older, Jersey City, 1860.............	54
XVIII	Presidential Election Returns, Jersey City, New Jersey, and United States......	58
XIX	City Missionary's Report, February, 1860...	65
XX	City Marshal's Report, November, 1860......	95
XXI	Election Returns for Recorder, Jersey City, 1861...............................	98
XXII	Jersey City Policemen by Nativity, 1860 and 1866............................	113
XXIII	Jersey City Policemen by Nativity, 1866 and 1870............................	129
XXIV	Jersey City Aldermen by Ethnicity, 1857, 1867, 1869.........................	140
XXV	Jersey City Aldermen by Ethnicity and Area, 1870............................	157

LIST OF MAPS

MAP   PAGE

I   Ward Boundaries, Jersey City, 1870..........   148

II District Boundaries, Jersey City, 1871......   206

CHAPTER I

INTRODUCTION

In 1850 Jersey City, a residential suburb of New York City, was governed by native-born Protestant members of the city's economic elite. By 1880 it had become an urban center of transportation and industry, governed largely by Irish Catholics of working class and lower middle class background. This important political transition followed changes in the city's underlying population from native-born to immigrant, from Protestant to Catholic, from predominantly middle and upper class to largely working and lower middle class. Although the population changed most radically in the 1850's, the shift in political power occurred two decades later--during the 1870's. For a quarter of a century native-born Protestants resisted immigrant penetration of the city's institutions and through a variety of devices succeeded in delaying what appeared inevitable.

At issue was a question of culture. The native-born Protestants who constituted the city's elite dreaded the prospect of a city dominated by Catholic immigrants. Defining themselves in terms of the values and mores of American Protestantism with its nearly pathological horror of "Romanism," native-born citizens worked to defend a way of life that an alien presence was rapidly undermining. The Irish symbolized a radically different culture, combining peasant values with Catholic religion.

In Jersey City, as in America generally, native-born citizens worked to change the Irish: to make them temperate, respectful of the Sabbath, and if possible even Protestant. The Irish, on the other hand, resisted such coercive attempts at assimilation and sought to defend both their Irish identity and their Catholicism. Patrick Ford, the editor of the New York *Irish World*, correctly described the tension and conflict in 1872:

> Our lot is cast among a people who hate our nationality--a people who would absorb us if they cannot prevent our growth. How shall we preserve our identity? How shall we perpetuate our faith and nationality, through our posterity, and leave our impress on the civilization of this country as the puritans have?[1]

Eight years later the *Irish American* urged its readers to learn Gaelic, for "it means you will feel more proud and manly as Irishmen, and be more respected as American citizens."[2]

Such symbolic attainments as Gaelic were difficult for the Irish, however; as a group, the Irish were poor. The demographic analysis in Chapter II demonstrates a clear relationship between class, ethnicity, and religion in Jersey City in 1860. Irish poverty, however, was hardly understood, much less sympathized with, by native-born Protestants. In 1854 the *Irish American* blamed Irish "criminality" and drunkenness on "the vicissitudes of sorrow and poverty, . . . unemployment, &c.," that beset the Irish laboring population. But the editor of the <u>Daily Sentinel</u> in Jersey City scorned and ridiculed such ideas. "No Irishman ever died of hard work in America," he sneered. He even wagered that the "average" Yankee worked twice as hard as the "average" Irish man. Irish poverty had three causes. The Irish drank. The Irish "herd/ed7 and grovel/ed7 in crowded cities where labor is always in excess and bitterly competitive." And finally, the Catholic doctrine of Purgatory prevented them from internalizing the Protestant ethic and raising themselves up through fear of the Devil's bootstraps. In short, the Irish could cure their problems by ceasing to be Irish.[3]

Jersey City's native-born population attempted to change Irish identity. Through the 1850's they gave heavy support to such organizations as the City Mission and Tract Society and the Hudson County Bible Society. Know-Nothingism had strong appeal, and the management of schools, jails, and the poor house reflected widespread anti-Catholic sentiment. These efforts to force cultural changes--termed moral reforms by the participants--failed. Resistance, continued immigration, and poverty left the Irish community as distinct in 1860 as it had been in 1850. In the meantime, however, the Irish began to gain political recognition. During the decade of the 1860's the Irish attained elective office, first as the agents of native-born politicians and then in more independent ways. These small successes, not surprisingly, nurtured the anti-Catholicism and nativism of the 1850's which continued less overt in form but undiminished in intensity. When the Irish elected sympathetic men as city judge and city police chief, for example, the native-born elite convinced a cooperative state legislature to make these offices non-elective. After the Jersey City voters elected nearly all immigrants as city officials in 1870, fearful native-born citizens, Republicans and Democrats alike, created a charter that turned the powers of local government over to commissioners appointed by the state legislature. In many ways the high tide of nativism, commission government lasted for six years, from 1871 to 1877. Only after the commissions were repealed in 1877 did Jersey City's Catholic immigrant population attain the political power that their numbers in the city had so long warranted.

Most importantly, the nativism and anti-Catholicism that dominated middle class Protestant thought before the Civil War remained alive through and after it. While it was no longer an explicit national movement as in the 1850's, nativism at the local level did not end with the advent of war. There were other "irrepressible conflicts" in nineteenth century America, although their eruptions were hardly as sensational. The Civil War certainly diverted attention from the specter of "Romanism" rampant in the land, but anti-Catholics continued to see Catholicism as a clear, if not a present, danger, and worked to prevent increases in Catholic influence during as well as after the war. A Jersey City clergyman, fresh from missionary endeavors in Ceylon, connected the war itself with anti-Catholicism. "Make citizens of the Negro," preached the Rev. Henry M. Scudder in May 1865, "and the Hibernian element goes to the wall."[4] The movements in most large cities to reduce the number of elective offices were directly connected with anti-Catholicism, and if Jersey City was a typical case, were directed by former Know-Nothings.[*] Because of its organization, the historiography of nativism has missed the continuities that connected pre- and post-Civil War nativism. Ray Allen Billington's The Protestant Crusade covers 1800 to 1860, while John Higham's Strangers in the Land covers 1860 to 1925, without establishing a continuity with the earlier period.[5] Calling his chapter on the post-Civil War period "The Age of Confidence," Higham assumes that the absence of nationally organized nativist activity implied an absence of nativist feeling among individuals. While both The Protestant Crusade and Strangers in the Land are excellent books, by

---

[*]See chapters IV and VII, below.

accepting the Civil War as the critical dividing point in nineteenth century American history, they over-estimate the effect of the war on such currents as anti-Catholicism and nativism. Ethnic relations in Jersey City during the period 1850-1877 can be placed in their proper perspective only if the Civil War, as an issue, is ignored.

The events of 1850-1877 also must be understood in terms of the city's earlier history. In 1800, when New York City had a population of sixty thousand, the area that became Jersey City had a population of exactly thirteen, all residents of a single building that served as ferry house, farm house, and tavern.[6] Hardly a natural city site, the terrain consisted of a few hillocks surrounded by swamp and tidal mud flats on the west bank of the Hudson River. The site had but a single redeeming virtue: it was directly opposite New York City. From its beginnings in 1804, Jersey City remained a social and economic satellite of New York City.

Called Paulus Hook, these few hillocks extended into the Hudson, separating two broad shallow coves that lapped the Jersey shore. Beyond them was a swamp, and beyond that, Bergen Hill, the southern end of the Palisades, here only a steep ridge. The whole was a part of the township of Bergen, and the land on top of the hill was farmed by the descendants of the original Dutch settlers.[7] In 1804

the state granted a charter to the Associates of the
Jersey Company, who had bought Paulus Hook and the ferry
rights to Manhattan, to build a town. Expecting to profit
from land speculation, the Associates laid out a village
and then tried to sell their swamp lots to New York merchants, using the argument that to live in Jersey and commute on the ferry would be cheaper and easier than living
in New York City. But the terrain, title disputes, and
the community's semi-proprietary nature all discouraged
settlement. Twenty-five years later, in 1829, the community held only thirteen hundred people.[8]

Jersey City's growth paralleled New York's. As the
distance between New York's residential and business districts increased, many New York merchants found it convenient and desirable to live in Jersey City or Brooklyn
and commute between the two. After the Associates established night ferry service between Manhattan and Jersey
City in 1834, land values and building activity in Jersey
City increased greatly. The city grew as a satellite of
New York, a suburb of people who could afford the twenty-five cents a day demanded by the ferry monopoly. In an
age of water transportation, the Hudson River provided a
link between home and work that land transport did not yet
provide. Population doubled from thirteen hundred to
twenty-five hundred between 1830 and 1840. When the com-

munity received a municipal charter in 1838, the Associates' influence over community development diminished markedly, effectively ending the community's semi-proprietary nature.[9]

While the city's proximity to New York made it an attractive residential suburb, this same proximity eventually turned the city into a major transportation center. By 1875 every trunk line railroad except the New York Central had located its eastern terminus in Jersey City, across the unbridgeable Hudson from New York. Requiring large amounts of unskilled labor, the railroads transformed this New Jersey suburb. A new population, largely immigrant and poor, radically altered the city's nature. By 1860 Jersey City was sixty percent immigrant, and immigrants constituted 90% of the unskilled labor force.

Jersey City did not begin to become a major railroad center, however, until after 1850. Relying at first on water connections wherever possible, the early railroads made no effort to locate opposite Manhattan. The Erie Railroad, for example, ran east and west from Dunkirk, New York, to Piermont, New York, sixty miles up the Hudson from New York City. Similarly, the Camden and Amboy connected New York and Philadelphia by using water transport from New York City to Amboy, New Jersey, and then following the shortest land route to Camden, across the

Delaware from Philadelphia. Only when rail transport had
clearly demonstrated its superiority to water did railroads abandon their water lines and attempt to concentrate
opposite New York. The Erie transferred its operation
from Piermont to Jersey City between 1853 and 1861, and
the Camden and Amboy (bought out by the Pennsylvania in
1870) did the same soon after. Locating in Jersey City
presented certain problems. Bergen Hill had to be tun-
neled or cut, and the mud flats along the Hudson's west
shore had to be filled in to provide deep water dock facilities. During the same years that Jersey City's population
changed from native-born to immigrant, its shore line
moved a quarter of a mile out into the Hudson, decidedly
changing the nature of the landscape.* By 1873 the railroads owned virtually the entire Jersey City waterfront.[10]

    Excellent rail facilities as well as proximity to New
York City provided the impetus for industrial development.
Although glass, pottery, and soap-making industries had
been started in the 1820's and a small iron industry developed after 1845, industrial expansion did not begin until the city became New York's major railroad terminus.

---

*The resistance to this change on the part of all seg-
ments of the population was an important part of Jersey
City's social history and deserves serious treatment. It
is touched on here, however, only when relevant to the
theme of ethnic conflict.

In 1865 the United States Watch Company built a large factory and eleven years later the Lorillard tobacco company moved its entire New York facilities to Jersey City, building a factory that employed three thousand people, nearly all women and children.[11]

By 1870 industry and railroads had not only changed the character of the city's population but had also changed the city's physical environment. Railroads had cut through residential neighborhoods and had moved the shore line further and further away. A *New York Times* reporter visited Jersey City in 1870 and described the view that residents of a block called "Quality Row" once had looked out upon:

> In their best days no buildings stood between these houses and the bay, and a greensward extended down to the shore. Those of the old residents who still remain here speak with affectionate regret of the gilded spires, and snowy sails; the picture framed in by the dark blue outlines of the island hills; of delicious breezes that came from the ocean, and rippled the bay in their course; of the glory of moonlight and starlight, whose enchantment was as complete as it was fleeting,--all gone, to return no more forever, before the usurpations of trade.

From here the reporter walked along the shore and described what he saw in 1870:

> . . . a walk up to the Long Dock discloses, after you pass large manufactories, oil refineries, &c., that occupy nearly the entire space of dry land, the slimiest, dirtiest shore in this part of the country. When the tide is down, on a hot day, it is absolutely sickening. Old bits of carpet and

> clothing, ragged baskets, old tin kettles, bottles, and various articles of household crockery, all covered by green slime, are to be seen, suggestive of every nasty thing that lies or crawls in such a stench, including dead cats and dogs, and some other dread shapes whose mystery the rising and falling tides reveals. Decaying hulks of vessels are moored in the mud, where rats rush frantically through their gaping seams.[12]

These changes in the city's purpose had brought a cleavage in the city's population. By 1860 Jersey City was an immigrant, working class city with a sizable population that knew only "black, smoky machine shops, tumble-down houses, foundries, dirty streets, mud, filth, marsh, swarms of unwashed children, and crowds of whooping carters." Here were many of the city's immigrants--mostly Irish, but with some Germans and British--and a few native-born. Other parts of the city contained "long rows of compact blocks of brick houses, of uniform architecture, set back from the sidewalk, with beautiful patterns of flowers in front--nothing garish, but all clean, neat, and very comfortable."[13] Here was a population that was native-born, Protestant, and uneasy about the social changes taking place around it. We examine first the 1860 population, especially its ethnic, class, and religious characteristics, and then consider in detail the dynamic interaction between the competing ethnic groups, concentrating in particular on the native-born and the Irish. The religious, economic and social differences between these two groups, together almost eighty percent of the population in 1860, dominated the social history of Jersey City for over a quarter of a century.

DOCUMENTATION: CHAPTER I

[1] *Irish World* (New York), February 10, 1872.

[2] *Irish American* (New York), November 23, 1878.

[3] *Daily Sentinel and Advertiser* (Jersey City), August 22, 1854.

[4] *New York Times*, May 10, 1865.

[5] Ray Allen Billington, *The Protestant Crusade 1800-1860* (Quadrangle ed., Chicago, 1964); John Higham, *Strangers in the Land: Patterns of Nativism, 1860-1925* (Atheneum ed., New York, 1963).

[6] Alexander McLean, *History of Jersey City, N. J.* (Jersey City, 1894), pp. 20-32; Rev. Charles K. Imbrie, *History of the First Presbyterian Church of Jersey City, New Jersey* (New York, 1888), pp. 12-18.

[7] McLean, pp. 28-32; William E. Sackett, *Modern Battles of Trenton: 1868-1894*, Vol. I (Trenton, 1895), pp. 26-30.

[8] McLean, p. 34.

[9] Ibid., p. 38.

[10] *Evening Journal* (Jersey City), December 24, 1872 (hereafter cited as *Journal*).

[11] William H. Shaw, *History of Essex and Hudson Counties, New Jersey*, Vol. II (Philadelphia, 1884), pp. 1150-1161.

[12] *New York Times*, August 21, 1870.

[13] Ibid.

CHAPTER II

THE 1860 JERSEY CITY CENSUS

By 1860 the majority of Jersey City's adult population was foreign-born. Almost exclusively from Ireland, Great Britain (including Canada), and Germany, each group displayed clear occupational patterns that helped to define its place in the community. Because social class and ethnicity were closely related in Jersey City, careful examination of these links is essential to comprehend that city's social history. Political and social conflicts between 1850 and 1877 largely reflected these ethnic, class, and religious differences. It is important, therefore, to examine the dominant Jersey City ethnic groups and their relationship to one another before analyzing the social and political conflicts themselves.

We approach the city's population through the 1860 manuscript census. While there is no tool superior to the decennial census for a demographic and social portrait of Jersey City at this time, there were certain weaknesses in the 1860 census, both in the data gathered and in the means of gathering, which compromised its accuracy. Census-taking was not a highly developed art in 1860. Men deputized as Assistant United States Marshals canvassed the city, receiving two cents for each person enumerated. Reviewing the 1860 census ten years later, the New York Times reported that assistant marshals, "deeming their pay inadequate, were apt to slur over the returns, omitting many returns that involved time or trouble in the gathering." Additionally, the political nature of the appointments--coupled with the low pay--meant that "the great number" of enumerators "were found to be unable to carry out the work intelligibly."[1] The amount of time over which the count continued--more than six months in some places--meant that in a mobile population some saw the census-taker twice and others not at all. Not all those who received a visit from an enumerator made him welcome; householders did not take kindly to prying strangers. The questions were "inquisitorial," and although enumerators were told to "strive in every way" not to give even "the appearance of obtrusiveness," they found the citizenry often uncooperative.[2] A Jersey City newspaper commented on "the ignorance and peevishness" of the people and on their reluctance to part with the names and ages of their children.[3] Marshals were often confused with tax assessors, or at least respondents suspected that their answers might be used against them. Information on property ownership, therefore, was often understated.[4] Using the census as a guide, one could confuse some of Jersey City's wealthiest men with paupers. "Among the rich," reported the New York Times, "some of the questions are regarded as impertinent, and among the poor as frivolous, and incorrect answers are often given."[5]

In 1875, before the New York State census began, the _New York Irish American_ urged its readers to cooperate with the enumerators in order to increase the Assembly delegation of the city, assuring its readers that "this Census has no reference, whatever, to taxation, military service, or liability to jury duty," and that all responses would be kept "inviolably secret."[6]

Language and culture presented additional problems. Information often had to be elicited from English-speaking children in German families, and the responses, claimed the _New York Times_, were "often of a nature that leaves doubt as to the questions being understood." A Jersey City editor, aware of past problems, urged the appointment of at least one German-speaking enumerator in 1870.[7] Cultural biases also prevented full communication. For example, an anonymous enumerator revealed as much about himself as about Irish-born Charles Golden, who kept a liquor store in Jersey City's third ward, when he listed Golden's occupation as "Rum Hole."[8]

People were left out of the 1860 census altogether, either because of the lack of a scientific approach on the part of the marshals or because of an unwillingness on the part of a reluctant citizenry to cooperate. The 1870 Paterson census, for example, turned up only 6072 children of school age, a year after the city assessors had counted 8002. "Numerous families," reported the <u>New York Herald</u>, "complain that they have seen nothing of the census takers at all."[9] In compiling the 1856 Jersey City directory, William Gopsill wrote a short introduction describing his problems in gathering the necessary information. In some cases, his canvassers could not get beyond the "ignorant and impertinent domestics" who answered the door; in other cases, names were refused "for fear the parties might be called upon for one dollar and fifty cents School tax." Gopsill peremptorily dismissed these methodological problems with thoughts many census marshals probably shared: "<u>The names of such will not be greatly missed</u>."[10]

The accuracy of the census, then, raises large, but not insurmountable problems. Some people were missed, some refused to cooperate, and others hid their assets. For the 29,226 persons listed, however--the overwhelming majority of Jersey City's inhabitants--this is the one document that presents consistent social data. It is therefore unlikely that greater census accuracy would materially affect the following conclusions.

When the census marshal knocked in 1860, he asked the name, age, sex, occupation, and place of birth of all members of the family. He also inquired as to the value of all real and personal property of one hundred dollars or more, if children had attended school within the past year, and if any family members were insane, idiotic, or had married within the year. He did not ask other potentially useful questions. Although the household was the basic unit for enumeration purposes, the head of household was not specified, nor were other intra-household relationships stated. Internal evidence must frequently be relied upon to establish family relationships, but beyond the nuclear family, relationships often defy reconstruction. The census was preeminently an enumeration of people for the correct apportionment of Congress; the gathering of social statistics was in its infancy.

The primary social data gathered dealt with ethnicity and occupation. Our initial analysis will focus on the relationship between these two. In 1860, Jersey City was clearly an immigrant city (see Table I). Less than 40% of the adult males were native-born, and an almost equal

TABLE I

ALL WHITE MALES TWENTY AND OLDER, BY ETHNICITY, JERSEY CITY, 1860

	N	%
Native-born	2818	39.2
Irish	2636	36.7
British	918	12.8
German	810	11.3
TOTAL	7182	100.0%

number were Irish-born. The rest were almost evenly divided between the British (including Welsh, Scots, and Canadian) and the Germans, each of whom constituted just over 10% of the adult male population.*

Each of these groups, however, had a thoroughly distinctive social and occupational structure. By combining occupational and ethnic data, this fact becomes clear. The resulting over-all pattern reveals a city with most of the wealth and "respectability" on one side of an ethnic and religious divide, and most of the poor on another. This disparity in occupational structure between the two largest ethnic blocs, the native-born and the Irish, was, as will be developed in subsequent chapters, the single most important social fact uncovered in this Jersey City social profile.

For purposes of analysis, occupations have been divided into eight large categories based on levels of skill and kinds of work. While occupational title alone is a crude way to establish with precision an individual's social class, the pattern for each ethnic group based on just this data is so strikingly clear that more precise refinement is unnecessary for purposes of the analysis which follows. Three categories contained only non-workers. "Economic elite" occupations included merchants,

---
*As the occupations open to women were almost exclusively menial, our analysis of ethnicity and occupation will be confined to the male population.

brokers, bankers, manufacturers, and contractors. On a similar level were the professionals--doctors, lawyers, and clergymen. Below them, but still outside of the working class, were the white-collar workers: the clerks, bookkeepers, accountants, and salesmen. Skilled workers fell into two separate categories: artisans, including coopers, shoemakers, machinists, and wheelwrights, and workers in the building trades. And finally, below them, were the unskilled: mostly day laborers, porters, teamsters, and factory operatives. These men, the lowest paid, constituted the bottom of the socio-economic pyramid. Specific occupations of laborers seldom were listed, and although many laborers had permanent work as railroad freight handlers and yardmen, it is not possible to draw the important distinction between the regularly and the casually employed. Two additional categories, both above unskilled labor, fit less precisely into a hierarchy based largely on skill. Shop-keepers included grocers, druggists, saloon-keepers, and other small proprietors. Lastly there were public employees, less than one percent of the whole. About half were policemen, and most of the rest were post office clerks and customs inspectors.

The occupational pattern of the entire city and the profile of each ethnic group within that pattern is provided in Table II. No two ethnic groups have a profile

TABLE II

OCCUPATIONS BY NATIVITY OF ALL JERSEY CITY MALES, TWENTY AND OLDER, 1860

Occupation	Native		Irish		British		German		Total Men	
	N	%	N	%	N	%	N	%	N	%
Economic elite	470	16.7	61	2.3	83	9.0	47	5.8	661	9.2
Professional	140	5.0	9	.3	18	2.0	13	1.6	180	2.5
White-collar	570	20.2	98	3.7	135	14.7	50	6.2	853	11.9
Shop-keepers	167	5.9	131	5.0	45	4.9	86	10.6	429	6.0
Artisan	728	25.8	482	18.3	365	39.8	413	51.0	1988	27.7
Building trades	241	8.6	261	9.9	133	14.5	69	8.5	704	9.8
Unskilled	254	9.0	1472	55.9	106	11.5	109	13.4	1941	27.0
Government	47	1.7	13	.5	7	.8	0	0.0	67	0.9
No occupation	201	7.1	109	4.1	26	2.8	23	2.9	359	5.0
TOTAL	2818	100.0%	2636	100.0%	918	100.0%	810	100.0%	7182	100.0%

that is even superficially similar. Each group clustered into different categories. The native-born were the city's elite, the Irish were the city's poor, and the Germans and British were disproportionately clustered in the skilled trades. Grouping similar categories and eliminating others allows us to see these clusters still more clearly (see Table III); the relative wealth of the native-born and the poverty of the Irish are starkly highlighted.*

TABLE III

SELECTED JERSEY CITY OCCUPATIONS, BY ETHNICITY, WHITE MALES TWENTY AND OLDER, 1860

Occupation	Native N	%	Irish N	%	British N	%	German N	%
Non-workers	1180	42.1	168	6.6	236	25.7	110	13.6
Skilled	969	34.4	743	28.2	498	54.3	482	60.3
Unskilled	254	9.0	1472	55.9	106	11.5	109	13.8

Clearly, the native-born were the economic elite in Jersey City. Over 40% were either in elite occupations, the professions, or white-collar jobs. This group supplied the city, at least until the mid-1860's, with its political as well as its social and economic leadership. Virtually all Protestant in religion, this group of native-born non-

---

*Economic elite, professional, and white-collar occupations have been grouped as "Non-workers;" artisans and men in the building trades as "Skilled." Third, are the "Unskilled."

workers saw itself as the community's "natural" elite. Representing fully 42% of the city's native-born males, they nevertheless only constituted 16% of the city's adult male population. Social conflicts after 1860 involved challenges to the native-born elite's earlier hegemony.

To a great extent, this native-born elite did not work in Jersey City. Not only an industrial immigrant city, Jersey City was also a bedroom suburb of New York City. Living in single-dwelling row-houses on long, narrow plots of land, these men commuted each day on the ferries to Manhattan, paying twelve and a half cents each way for the privilege. According to the 1860 city directory, about 16% of the city's work force worked in New York City, mostly as merchants, clerks, or successful restauranteurs. Because of the city's occupational structure, the commuters were overwhelmingly native-born.

Jersey City's economic elite, then, were not uniformly tied to that city's economy. Its members had rejected living in an industrial, immigrant city, such as New York City. Further, Jersey City's economic elite were not part of an older resident elite. The place had been but a village in 1840, so the elite themselves were migrant. Among native-born merchants, for example, only 28% were born in New Jersey, while 44% came from New York and 18% from New England. The fourteen native-born aldermen who served during 1857-1858 reflected this diversity. Only one, the son of a British immigrant, was born in Jersey City, and only three others came from New Jersey. Six were from New York, divided equally between the city and upstate, and the rest came from New England and other areas of the northeast.

Another 35% of the native-born were skilled workers, working in small shops and factories or for the railroads. Undoubtedly the city's largest employers, the railroads[*] were excluded from the census of manufactures, and railroad workers, as such, were not designated in the manuscript census. A large proportion of the city's skilled workers, however, found employment in the railroad repair shops and other facilities. If not, strictly speaking, factory workers, they nevertheless worked under industrial conditions. Only 9.0% of the native-born were unskilled workers, although unskilled workers constituted over a quarter of the city's work force (see Table II). The native-born white population, therefore, was relatively and absolutely affluent, and its members' living standards ranged from the modest comforts provided by a skilled laborer's wages to the opulence of the successful New York merchants.

---

[*]In 1860 the most important railroads were the Erie, the Morris and Essex, and the New Jersey Railroad.

The Irish related to the city in a nearly opposite manner. Largely unskilled, 56% of the Irish adult males were among the working poor. Some were cartmen, unskilled factory operatives, and day laborers. A large percentage worked for the railroads, especially on track maintenance and on the freight docks. They populated the newly rising tenements along the waterfront and the shanties that dotted the swampy areas of the city. The Irish were poor. A mere 28% were skilled workers; only among the Irish did the number of unskilled men in the working class exceed the number of skilled men. Among the native-born, the British, and the Germans, the working class was three-fourths skilled, but among the Irish it was two-thirds unskilled. An Irish elite hardly existed--a mere 6.3% of the men held elite occupations, had professions, or did white-collar work. Further, the Irish were divided into Protestant and Catholic, with the Protestants constituting perhaps 10% of the total. How religious affiliation cut across class lines is not evident from the census. But since three of the city's nine Irish professionals were Protestant ministers, it seems likely that the Catholic elite were even fewer than 6.0% of the Irish population. Not surprisingly, given the relative poverty of the Irish community, the Alms House in 1860 had thirty-seven adult Irish residents out of a total adult population of forty-five.

The German elite and white-collar group was also small, but made up a significantly larger percentage of the German community (13.6%) than the Irish elite did of theirs. While there were few wealthy Germans, there were also very few poor. Only 13.4% of the German men were unskilled. A full 59.5% were skilled workers, and another 10.6% were shop-keepers. Here was the key to the German community: it was prosperous without being wealthy; Germans had emigrated with skills that could be utilized after arrival. Not a German lived in the Alms House; the German population was apparently sufficiently prosperous to support its unfortunates without recourse to public institutions.[11]

Of the immigrant groups, the British were clearly the most prosperous. More than 25% of adult British males were outside the working class and another 54.3% in the skilled trades, leaving only 11.5% as unskilled, a figure only slightly higher than that of the native-born. English-speaking and not conspicuously poor, Jersey City's British population blended into the native-born community with relative ease.* Jersey City's editors were unaware that

---
*Some of those listing their place of birth as England were, culturally, Irish. The 1851 British census uncovered over 500,000 people of Irish birth in England, and there was a steady migration of Irishmen from England to America. Children born in England of Irish parents were listed in the United States census as English-born. The family of Hugh Killin, a laborer, provides an example. Born in Ireland (as was his wife, Bridget), their three

the second largest immigrant group in the city were the British, not the Germans. Because of the ease with which they were accepted, British immigrants played a role in Jersey City's subsequent history far out of proportion to their numbers.

The relationship between class and ethnicity becomes even clearer if certain occupational categories are analyzed in terms of their ethnic complexion (see Table IV). The upper class, for example, was almost 70% native-born,

TABLE IV

NATIVITY BY SELECTED OCCUPATIONS,
WHITE MALES TWENTY AND OLDER, JERSEY CITY, 1860

	Non-worker (1694)	Skilled (2679)	Unskilled (1941)	Total (6314)
Native-born	69.7%	36.0%	13.1%	38.1%
Irish	9.9	27.6	75.9	37.7
British	13.9	18.5	5.5	13.1
German	6.5	17.9	5.5	11.1
TOTAL	100.0%	100.0%	100.0%	100.0%

while the Irish constituted 75% of the unskilled. Only among the skilled laborers did the proportion of each ethnic group even approximate the distribution of each group in the total male population--and even here the Irish were

older children, ranging in age from fifteen to eleven, were born in England. The next three were born in the United States, one in Connecticut and two in New Jersey. If the older children had their own households in 1870, as is likely, they appeared in that census as English-born--as did a number of English-born "Irishmen" in 1860.

somewhat under-represented. Were there no relationship between class and ethnicity, then the figures in the first three columns of Table IV would approximate those in column four.

These patterns relating class to ethnicity are reinforced by the 1860 census data on real property ownership (see Table V). Focusing on the native-born and the Irish in the fourth ward, we find that the native-born

TABLE V

REAL PROPERTY OWNED BY NATIVE-BORN AND IRISH
FOURTH WARD, JERSEY CITY, 1860

Native-born: Entire ward and selected occupations

	Number of men	Number owning property	% owning property
Entire ward	929	242	26.0
Non-worker	354	116	34.6
Skilled	379	77	20.3
Unskilled	72	11	7.5

Irish: Entire ward and selected occupations

	Number of men	Number owning property	% owning property
Entire ward	634	79	12.5
Non-worker	47	18	38.3
Skilled	192	24	12.5
Unskilled	346	26	7.5

were more than twice as likely to own real property as the Irish. Further, within specific occupational categories (except for the small group outside the working class), the Irish were less than half as likely to report real property as were the native-born. Among skilled and unskilled workers in both groups, over 90% of those reporting property reported no more than five thousand dollars worth, indicating home ownership. Irish workers at all skill levels, we can conclude, were less than half as likely to own homes as their native-born counterparts.

Most property in the fourth ward, however, was not owned by workers. Among the 242 native-born property owners, nineteen owned 69.3% of all real estate reported, in amounts ranging from $25,000 to $430,000. These men were largely the descendents of the original Dutch farmers, now managing blocks of tenements where they had formerly grown food crops for the New York market. Only three Irish men owned property worth $25,000, and none reported more than $40,000.

Jersey City had one other ethnic group: the small community of native-born Negroes. Clearly less well off than the city's Irish, the eighty Negro males were uniformly in the working class and almost all unskilled (see Table VI). The skilled workers included a barber, a

TABLE VI

OCCUPATIONS OF NEGRO MALES, TWENTY AND OLDER, JERSEY CITY, 1860

	$\underline{N}$	%
Artisans	5	6.2
Building trades	2	2.5
Unskilled	69	86.3
No occupation	4	5.0
TOTAL	80	100.0%

musician, a baker, two carpenters, a refiner, and an engineer. Twenty of the unskilled were common laborers, fourteen seamen, and sixteen waiters or servants. Only four blacks reported real property, in amounts varying from five hundred to three thousand dollars. This "gentry" consisted of two laborers, a cartman, and the engineer.

In addition to enumerating the population, the census-takers visited every manufacturing establishment producing more than five hundred dollars worth of goods annually, and inquired into capitalization, the number and sex of employees, total monthly wages, and the value of the goods produced. The manuscript census of manufactures allows us to reconstruct certain aspects of industrial employment in Jersey City. Most industrial units were small, typically employing under twenty-five men (see Table VII). Although only a third of the factories employed over

TABLE VII

SIZE OF INDUSTRIAL UNITS BY NUMBER OF WORKERS, JERSEY CITY, 1860

Number employed	Number of factories		Number of workers	
1 - 9	29	38.7%	141	9.2%
10 - 24	23	30.7	338	22.1
25 - 49	13	17.3	417	27.3
50 - 74	7	9.3	409	26.7
75 - 90	3	4.0	225	14.7
	75	100.0%	1530	100.0%

twenty-five workers, this third employed 68.7% of Jersey

City's industrial workers. Typically, factory employees worked in relatively large industrial units. Jersey City's factory operatives were very much subject to the patterns and disciplines of industrialization that emerged in the mid-nineteenth century. The revolution in work patterns was incomplete in 1860, and no factory employed over ninety people. Employment under industrial conditions was probably most pronounced in the railroad facilities, a facet of Jersey City's economy not articulated in the census. We can glimpse this world through the 1870 industrial census. Perhaps by error, the 1870 census of manufactures included the Erie repair shops. In 1870 these two shops, in existence in 1860, employed 997 men, almost a third of all workers listed in the 1870 census of manufactures. As this was but one phase of the work of one railroad, the railroads must be considered the most important employers in Jersey City. In all probability a similar pattern prevailed in 1860, with the railroads employing large numbers of men under industrial conditions.

Jersey City's largest factories were ancillary to railroading. A railroad car factory and a steam engine factory, the city's largest, each employed ninety men. Closely related was the iron and steel industry. Half a dozen foundries turned out iron rails and steel plate for the local factories and for the nearby Paterson locomotive works. Older, but still important, were jewelry, pottery, and soap factories. Larger industrial units became much more common after 1860. In 1870 the newly built Mathiesson and Wiecher sugar works and the short-lived United States Watch factory each employed 350 workers; by 1880 fifteen establishments each employed over one hundred people, and the Lorrilard tobacco factory, built in 1876, employed 3475 workers.[12]

Examining selected skilled factory occupations allows us to penetrate some of the more subtle ethnic distinctions within the skilled labor class itself. Jewelers, machinists, and iron moulders were all skilled men. Among the highest paid artisans in the city, jewelers and machinists were predominantly German and native-born (see Table VIII). Only among iron moulders, whose work was hot and dirty, were there many Irish. Reflecting their pre-

TABLE VIII

ETHNICITY OF SELECTED OCCUPATIONS, JERSEY CITY, 1860

	Jeweler (134)	Machinist (157)	Moulder (178)
Native-born	32.1%	43.3%	23.6%
Irish	2.2	25.5	45.5
British	16.4	9.6	25.3
German	49.3	21.6	5.6
TOTAL	100.0%	100.0%	100.0%

immigration industrial experience, many moulders were British. When James R. Thompson founded the Jersey City Steel Works in 1862, its actual manager had emigrated from

Sheffield; conversely, an early attempt to found a local moulders' union in 1860 was sparked by an English worker.[13] Unskilled factory labor was largely Irish. The Colgate Soap Company, for example, employed fifty men in Jersey City in 1860; of the thirty-two who can be identified from the manuscript census, twenty-five, or 78.2%, were Irish.

The work force did not consist solely of men over the age of twenty. Most males fifteen to nineteen worked, but the period was basically a time of transition into the labor force. It included many young men in occupations that would not prove to be their permanent calling. Because the employment pattern for men under twenty was somewhat different from that of older men, it deserves separate treatment. There were, for example, no merchants or brokers, but a full two-thirds of the employed native-born teenagers called themselves clerks. The term, however, could mean vastly different things. Some clerks filled ledgers with figures, others filled sacks with groceries. There is no way to distinguish them. That the number of clerks dropped sharply among men over twenty indicates that for many, especially among the native-born, time spent as a clerk was a period of preparation for entry into the mercantile community. A large number of young men were neither employed nor in school, but listed as living at home. A few undoubtedly took part in the youth gangs that roamed the city streets, such as the Lava Bed gang.[14] Others were perhaps partially employed or occasionally employed, but without a permanent job.

The occupational pattern for those in skilled and unskilled occupations resembled that of older men, but with some significant differences. Among all ethnic groups, the proportion of unskilled young men was less than among the older men, with the largest difference among the Irish (see Table IX). Although very few young

TABLE IX

OCCUPATION BY NATIVITY, MALES, 15 - 19,
JERSEY CITY, 1860

Occupation	Native N	%	Irish N	%	British N	%	German N	%
Clerk	168	39.2	32	8.6	27	19.7	8	9.4
Artisan	54	12.5	78	20.8	29	21.1	33	38.9
B'ding trades	13	3.0	22	5.9	15	11.0	3	3.5
Shop-keeper	8	1.9	5	1.3	0	0.0	2	2.4
Unskilled	18	4.2	116	30.9	14	10.2	7	8.2
Apprentice	15	3.5	29	7.7	15	11.0	7	8.2
Other*	8	1.9	3	.8	2	1.5	0	0.0
In school	62	14.5	37	9.9	18	13.1	6	7.0
No occupation	83	19.3	53	14.1	17	12.4	19	22.4
TOTAL	429	100.0%	375	100.0%	137	100.0%	85	100.0%

*"Other" includes two nineteen-year-old merchants and eight in various white-collar jobs.

men were in the building trades (about 5% of the whole), about a dozen others were listed as apprentices.

Although Jersey City had no public high school until 1872, having only introduced graded education in 1860, almost ten percent of the young men are listed as attending school, most of them aged fifteen or sixteen. The city did have a small number of private lyceums, both Protestant and Catholic, that offered post-primary education for those who could pay the tuition and felt the need, but few parents in any ethnic group kept their children in formal schooling beyond the age of fourteen. Few children fourteen or younger, however, worked. No industries in the city relied on child labor, and most employed boys appear to have worked either beside their fathers or as clerks. Only among the Irish were boys working at unskilled jobs unrelated to father's livelihood. Of fifty-five employed boys, thirty-two were Irish, and half of these worked as laborers or factory operatives. Even among the Irish, formal employment below fifteen appears to have been exceptional.

At least half of Jersey City's adult population was female. The majority of all adult women were married and did not work outside the home. They were wives and mothers, not members of the labor force. Just as few worked, few headed households, and almost none lived alone. We will examine closely all women in the fourth ward over the age of fifteen in terms of their relationship to family, employment, and formal education. We shall then look at employed women in the entire city, and finally at the large domestic servant population.

Because the 1860 census does not identify heads of households or the relationship of family members to each other, only a limited number of conclusions about families can be drawn. The nuclear family is readily distinguishable, as the general order of listing was adult male, adult female, and children. Non-nuclear families are more difficult to uncover. There is no way to distinguish augmented and extended families. With reasonable accuracy, we can identify five categories of women: wives, heads of households, daughters living at home, servants, and "others," either boarders or relatives. (As they cannot consistently be distinguished, they will be treated here as "boarders," an arbitrary designation.)

Employment data for women are extremely unreliable. Either the census-takers were more casual in their inquiries here, or respondents were reluctant to admit that their wives or daughters worked outside the home. One example will suffice. Jersey City had, in 1860, one factory that reported in the industrial census using eighty female workers. The census of persons, however, turned up exactly five females confessing to factory labor, a large and important discrepancy. The employment figures for women may tell us more about what people thought women should do than about what they in fact did.

Focusing on the life patterns of native-born and Irish women in the city's most populous ward, Table X re-

TABLE X

NATIVE-BORN AND IRISH WOMEN BY ROLE AND AGE,
FOURTH WARD, JERSEY CITY, 1860

Role	Native-born					
	15-19	20-29	30-39	40-49	50-59	60+
Wife at home, not working	8	245	252	103	48	12
Wife working	0	0	0	0	0	0
Head of household, not working	0	0	8	14	14	23
Head of household, working	0	3	3	1	1	4
Daughter at home, not working	84	78	13	2	1	0
Daughter at home, working	38	11	2	0	0	0
Daughter at home, in school	23	0	0	0	0	0
Boarder, not working	8	59	18	16	16	44
Boarder, working	3	11	1	0	0	0
Servant, living in	19	7	2	0	1	0
TOTAL	183	414	299	136	81	83

Role	Irish					
	15-19	20-29	30-39	40-49	50-59	60+
Wife at home, not working	8	178	189	77	15	10
Wife working	0	0	0	1	0	0
Head of household, not working	0	4	14	12	17	12
Head of household, working	0	2	5	2	2	0
Daughter at home, not working	29	10	0	0	0	0
Daughter at home, working	25	34	0	0	0	0
Daughter at home, in school	5	0	0	0	0	0
Boarder, not working	3	12	4	3	3	9
Boarder, working	2	4	0	0	0	0
Servant, living in	65	158	41	12	5	0
TOTAL	137	402	253	107	42	31

veals that the overwhelming majority of women over thirty in both ethnic groups were married, living with their husbands, and not in the labor force. The pattern for women under thirty differed sharply. The key factor here was work experience. As a rule, Irish women worked for at least part of the period between fifteen and thirty, and native-born women did not. Of those between fifteen and nineteen, 28.3% of the native-born women worked, compared with 67.1% of the Irish. Between ages twenty and twenty-nine, this cleavage became even more pronounced: while a mere 7.6% of the native-born women worked, 49.2% of the Irish worked, primarily as servants. As Jersey City Irish families were largely poor and the native-born were not, the percentage of unmarried Irish women in the labor force was a function of family poverty and the need for the wages of more than one family member. Returning to women fifteen to nineteen, 68.4% of the native-born lived with their parents, and of that number, only 26.2% are reported as working. Among the Irish, on the other hand, only 43.1% lived at home, and of these 42.4% worked. If Irish girls spent their afternoons in comfortable drawing rooms, it was with feather dusters rather than needle-point.

Very few German women were reported as working. Their absence may possibly be a result of language difficulties in taking the census, but more probably is attributable to the tendency of German women to marry earlier

than either their native-born or Irish counterparts. In
the fourth ward, for example, only seven German women over
twenty lived at home unmarried. Among the Germans, the
number of men exceeded the number of women. Furthermore,
the large number of skilled workers among the male work
force enabled families to support themselves with one income.

While unmarried Irish women worked, married women
clearly did not. In the fourth ward, no native-born married woman, and only one Irish woman, reported employment.
Although this probably understates the number of employed
married women, very clearly removal from the work force
came with marriage. Similarly, few women headed households after marriage. Although each ethnic group in Jersey
City had its own unique social structure, this did not
affect the distribution of two-parent households in any
statistically significant manner (see Table XI). Further,

TABLE XI

HEADS OF HOUSEHOLDS BY SEX,
FOURTH WARD, JERSEY CITY, 1860

	Native (769)	Irish (531)	British (255)	German (233)	Negro* (70)
Male	90.5%	86.8%	89.5%	96.1%	88.6%
Female	9.5	13.2	10.5	3.9	11.4

*Based on figures for the entire city.

the data on native-born and Irish women presented in

Table X shows that female heads of households were basically older women: widows rather than deserted wives or unmarried mothers.

From the woman as family member, we return to the woman as worker (see Table XII). Jobs for women were few in number and without status or high pay. Most women who

---

TABLE XII

OCCUPATIONS OF WHITE WOMEN, FIFTEEN AND OLDER, JERSEY CITY, 1860

	Native		Irish		British		German	
Occupation	N	%	N	%	N	%	N	%
Clothing trades*	108	39.9	251	19.1	71	49.3	21	23.7
Boarding house	6	2.2	10	.8	4	2.7	1	1.2
Store-kpr.	6	2.2	15	1.2	5	3.5	3	3.4
Teacher	25	9.1	4	.3	7	4.9	5	5.7
Nurse	8	3.0	7	.5	2	1.4	1	1.2
Factory	2	.7	3	.2	0	0.0	0	0.0
Servant	108	39.9	999	76.0	41	28.5	47	53.4
Other	8	3.0	25	1.9	14	9.7	10	11.4
TOTAL	271	100.0%	1314	100.0%	144	100.0%	88	100.0%

*"Clothing trades" includes tailoresses, dressmakers, seamstresses, milliners, and vestmakers.

---

escaped domestic service worked at some phase of sewing or tailoring, probably in the home; servants and clothing workers accounted for 91.1% of all women workers. A few ran small stores or kept boarders. A smaller number, largely native-born, taught school. Some reported occupations related to a family business; one jeweler used three daughters to make gold chain; another had a daughter working as a polisher. Although the census reported no prostitutes, two households in particular would appear to be houses of prostitution. In the first ward, six women under forty, all named Smith and giving their occupations as dressmakers, lived with a man who gave his occupation as salesman. In the fourth ward, a native-born woman with two children headed a household that also included eleven Irish "laundresses," all under thirty.

Most women who worked did so as domestic servants. They must be studied not only in terms of who they were, but also in terms of whom they worked for, as servants were members of the households in which they worked, and of necessity had a personal as well as a professional relationship with their employers. The servant population of Jersey City was over 80% Irish (see Table XIII) and young. Over 75% were below the age of thirty. While most

TABLE XIII

SERVANTS BY ETHNICITY AND AGE,
JERSEY CITY, 1860

	Under 15	15-19	20-29	30-39	40-49	50-69	Total	%
Native	11	49	28	13	4	3	108	8.8
Irish	24	175	594	161	30	15	999	81.9
British	3	8	20	5	1	4	41	3.4
German	2	15	28	0	1	1	47	3.9
Negro	1	7	7	1	3	3	25	2.0
TOTAL	41	254	677	180	39	26	1220	100.0%

servants were Irish, most families that employed servants were not. Reflecting their affluence, almost 80% of the families employing servants were native-born (see Table XIV). A pattern emerges here. Although the demand for servants was greatest among the native-born, each nationality employed servants of its own kind whenever possible.

TABLE XIV

SERVANTS AND EMPLOYERS BY ETHNICITY,
JERSEY CITY, 1860

Employers	Servants						
	Native	Irish	British	German	Negro	Total	%
Native	98	785	26	12	22	943	77.3
Irish	2	126	3	2	0	133	10.9
British	4	63	11	0	3	81	6.6
German	4	25	1	33	0	63	5.2
TOTAL	108	999	41	47	25	1220	100.0%

A quarter of the British servants worked for British households; almost three-fourths of the German women who worked as servants served German households; ninety percent of the native-born women worked in native-born households. The most important figure, however, is the 785 Irish servants in native-born households, accounting for two-thirds of all servants. These girls, almost all Catholic, worked in homes that were almost all Protestant. Jersey City had two daily papers, both strongly identified with nativism, and both editors had Irish servants living in their homes. We can only guess at the tensions and conflicts that cultural and religious differences between master and servant produced. A letter in the New York Times in 1853 captured the ambiguities of these relationships. The author asserted that Catholic domestics were "never compelled to attend . . . the family prayers . . . or even to keep the Sabbath, (the Lord forgive his people this sin,) which, according to the higher law, heads of families should require of them."[15]

Religion interacted with class and ethnicity in Jersey City, and religious conflict played a major role in the city's social development. After 1850 the Protestant elite became fully conscious that the poor among them were not only Irish but also Catholic. Although the federal census made no inquiries concerning religion, the City Mission and Tract Society and the Hudson County Bible Society undertook religious censuses of the community in 1856, 1865, and 1869.[16] The methods employed were amateurish and crude, and those taking the censuses met resistance among Catholics as members of Protestant proselytizing organizations; nevertheless, the data tended to confirm the census data linking class and ethnicity.

Each census organized the data in slightly different ways. Primarily concerned with the proportion of Catholics to Protestants, the censuses did not deal comprehensively with ethnicity. Germans, however, were enumerated separately in 1856 and 1865. The data demonstrated that by 1856 the fundamental change from a virtually all Protestant city to a city with a significant Catholic minority had already taken place (see Table XV). Over the next thirteen years, although the city's population almost doubled, the

TABLE XV

RELIGIOUS AFFILIATION BY FAMILY,
JERSEY CITY, 1856, 1865, 1869

	1856		1865		1869	
	Families	%	Families	%	Families	%
Protestant	3013	65.7	4508	62.7	5211	60.2
Catholic	1582	34.3	2649	36.7	3402	39.3
Jewish	0	0.0	56	.8	45	.5
TOTAL	4595	100.0%	7213	100.0%	8658	100.0%

proportion of Catholics rose from one-third to two-fifths. The absolute increase in the number of Catholics, however, more graphically describes the changes in the city's religious complexion than the relative increase. While the city grew 88.7%, the Protestant population increased by only 72.9%. But the Catholic population increased by 115.0%. Here, in 1869, was a statistic for Protestants to ponder.

The German population was basically Protestant, with Catholics constituting about a quarter of the total in 1856 and 1865, and Jews just under a tenth in 1865 (see Table XVI). That the German population was largely Protestant meant that the Catholic population was overwhelmingly Irish. German Catholics accounted for about five percent of the Catholic population in 1856 and again in 1865. When the data in Tables XV and XVI are compared with that in Table II, there is no mistaking the fact that not only was the Catholic church the church of the poor, it also was the only church of the poor.

TABLE XVI

RELIGIOUS AFFILIATION BY FAMILY,
JERSEY CITY GERMANS, 1856, 1865

	1856		1865	
	Families	%	Families	%
Protestant	262	76.4	428	67.4
Catholic	81	23.6	151	23.8
Jewish	0	0.0	56	8.8
TOTAL	343	100.0%	635	100.0%

The members of the Protestant elite who saw a "relationship" between poverty and religion were in a sense correct. Three-fourths of the unskilled laborers were Irish, and they made up over half of the Irish male population. Over four-fifths of the domestic servants were similarly Irish and almost all were also Catholic. As anti-Catholicism was one of the most important social and intellectual currents in nineteenth century America, the religious divisions in Jersey City compounded the social and ethnic divisions. Anti-Catholicism, anti-foreignism, and fear of the disorderly poor all blurred together in the minds of many native-born citizens, for the Catholic, the foreign, and the poor were to a great extent the same group of people.

DOCUMENTATION: CHAPTER II

[1] New York Times, August 14, 1870.

[2] Ibid.

[3] American Standard (Jersey City), August 13, 1860.

[4] New York Times, August 14, 1870. See also Edward Pessen, "The Egalitarian Myth and the American Social Reality: Wealth, Mobility, and Equality in the 'Era of the Common Man,'" American Historical Review, Vol. LXXVI, No. 4 (October, 1971), pp. 992-997.

[5] New York Times, August 14, 1870.

[6] Irish American, June 5, 1875.

[7] New York Times, August 14, 1870; Journal, April 4, 1870.

[8] This and the following census information is from the Federal manuscript census schedules of Jersey City, New Jersey, 1860. National Archives Microfilm Publication, Roll 653-693.

[9] New York Herald, September 16, 1870.

[10] Hudson County Courier, May 7 through June 25, 1857.

[11] A total of 54, or 6.7% of the Germans (0.8% of the whole), came from elsewhere in northern Europe. Over half of these, 33, were born in France, but most had distinctly German names. Also included are 11 from Holland and 1 from Belgium, 3 Poles, 2 Russians (one with a German wife), and 6 Swiss, all with German names. Excluded are 2 Italians (a seaman and a priest), and a Portuguese gardener.

[12] Shaw, Vol. II, p. 1159.

[13] Journal, May 22, 1868; American Standard, March 20, 1860.

[14] Augustine E. Costello, History of the Police Department of Jersey City (Jersey City, 1891), p. 227.

[15] New York Times, December 23, 1853.

16 William Verrinder, *Report of the City Missionary to the Board of Managers of the Jersey City Bible Society, February 20, 1857* (Jersey City, 1857), p. 13; *Jersey City Times*, December 11, 1865; November 5, 1869.

CHAPTER III

THE PROTESTANT CITY:
ASPECTS OF NATIVISM, 1850 - 1859

In 1854 the New Jersey Assembly appointed a three-man committee to study the desirability of passing resolutions urging that Congress increase the naturalization period from five to twenty-one years. The majority concluded the resolution unnecessary, but the minority member, John K. Roberts of Camden, recommended passage. He was troubled by changes taking place around him that threatened to remake the society he had known:

> Foreign tongues are heard on every hand. Foreign newspapers flood the country. Districts of foreigners, townships of foreigners, counties of foreigners, with foreign hearts, and foreign manners, and foreign institutions, dot the whole country. Foreign quarters are found in our cities, and bands of armed foreigners parade our streets with foreign insignia. Foreign priests employ the thunders of a foreign politico-religious power to force from the hands of legal trustees the property of American citizens.

Despite his strong rhetoric, Roberts approached the problem cautiously. He was unable to reconcile his image of America as a country open to all who came with the consequences of admitting those who held different social or religious ideals. While he would not curtail immigration, nor abridge the constitutional freedoms of immigrants, he would prevent the transference of political power to men unlike himself.

> Let the disciples of German infidelity condemn the Christian Sabbath, and English Radicals call down perdition upon the Constitution and the Father of his country, because the one recognizes compulsory servitude and the other held slaves. But let us not say to these men who are still aliens, "in five short years we will empower you, by law, to <u>act</u> upon these opinions in the political arena."[1]

Nowhere in New Jersey was the problem of immigrant influence greater than in Jersey City. A town of 11,500 in 1850, Jersey City grew to 21,000 in five years and to 30,000 in another five.[2] Much, if not most of this growth, was Irish, Catholic, and poor. Control of the city's institutions throughout the pre-Civil War period, however, remained firmly with the native-born elite, who were not unmindful of the threat posed to their hegemony by their alien neighbors. Through the municipal government and voluntary societies closely related to the government, the native-born worked hard to change immigrant values and behavior sufficiently to defuse this threat. The American, or Know-Nothing, party attracted perhaps as many as half of Jersey City's native-born voters in 1856, a strong expression of nativist sentiment. The Protestant churches worked hard to "de-Catholicize" the Irish and clearly perceived the political consequences of their actions. Like Assemblyman Roberts, when they discussed "Americanism" they did so largely in Protestant terms. It is no exaggeration, for the 1850's, to talk of Jersey City as a Protestant city, even if forty percent of its population was Catholic. An examination of selected but important aspects of the city's social history in the 1850's reveals the friction between rich and poor, native and immigrant, Protestant and Catholic. We focus on the city government, the Know-Nothing party, an Alms House dispute, and a strike of Irish laborers.

I

Local or municipal governmental power rested with the Board of Aldermen, four from each of the city's four wards, elected for two-year staggered terms. Through a system of committees they ran the alms house and prison, contracted for street repairs, approved or disapproved every expenditure of the school board (which they themselves appointed), and controlled the police department, both approving all expenditures and appointing the patrolmen. The mayor could approve or disapprove the measures passed, but his veto was easily over-ridden, and Jersey City mayors provided little leadership during the 1850's. Initiative lay with the aldermen, and the aldermen were almost exclusively native-born Protestants from the city's economic elite. The aldermen who took office in May 1857 were typical of the men who governed the city before the Civil War. Through May and June of 1857, the Hudson County Courier printed biographies of all sixteen, noting that increases and changes in the population made it impossible for all men to know their aldermen. The biographies appeared because the editor felt that a sense of community no longer existed, necessitating more formal ways of dispensing information.

Thirteen of the sixteen aldermen were native-born of native-born parents. Two were Irish, and one was of Irish parentage. Seven of the native-born members had occupations that placed them with the economic elite, and two others were professionals, both lawyers. Of the four remaining, three were store-keepers and one was a customs official, but this did not mean that they were poor men. Two of the store-keepers owned large amounts of real estate, one in excess of fifty thousand dollars, and the father of the customs officer was a wealthy New York merchant. As for the Irish aldermen, they were hardly typical of the city's Irish. Hugh McComb, a builder, left the Democratic party in 1856 over the slavery issue and was elected as a Republican. Richard Cornelison, although Irish-born and Catholic, was raised in Manchester, England, and had become foreman of a silk factory there. Worth $2500 when he emigrated in 1851, he immediately opened a dry goods and silk importing firm in New York. The sixteenth alderman, born to Irish parents in western New York, grew up in Ann Arbor, Michigan, where his father was a miller. After attending the University of Michigan, he migrated to New York City where he manufactured rubber and gutta-percha goods. None of the aldermen were poor; only one, a native-born store-keeper, could not be classed with the city's elite.[3]

In party affiliation, eleven were Democrats, three were Republicans, and two were Know-Nothings, both elected in 1856. While only two called themselves Know-Nothings, many more had ties to nativism and anti-Catholicism. William Roosevelt, for example, was a Democrat but, reported the Courier, was suspected of Know-Nothing sentiments by "the sounder portion of the democracy who swear 'vingeance to thim bloody Know-Nothings--bad luck to thim.'"[4] Matthew Erwin, another Democrat, was opposed by the Catholics in his ward because of his views on church taxation, and Robert Kashow's notions shop was the local Bible Society's book depository.[5] Nativism and anti-Catholicism rippled through the community in a variety of ways. A few joined the various secret societies, some supported the candidates of the American party, and others supported nativism in a social and religious sense if not in a political sense. Like Dudley S. Gregory, a Republican mayor from 1858 to 1860, they spoke of "the low Irish" who "voted according to prejudice and as their leaders dictated."[6]

II

As a result of the large foreign-born population in

Jersey City, the American party achieved a larger percentage of the vote in the 1856 presidential election than it did in either the state of New Jersey or in the nation as a whole. The party was well enough organized to support a small weekly newspaper, the <u>Hudson County Courier</u>, edited by William Dunning, a former Whig. As a prelude to the election, the American party planned a series of rallies to ratify the nominations of Millard Filmore for President and Andrew J. Donelson for Vice-President. A petition circulated through the city by the party elite in August 1856 drew the signatures of almost six hundred Filmore supporters, and the <u>Courier</u> printed the entire list.[7]

As these 591 men constituted 70% of the Know-Nothing vote in 1856, they provide a unique opportunity to study the social characteristics of the party's electorate in one city. When the occupational structure of the 473 men for whom data are available is compared to the structure for all native-born men aged twenty and over as it appeared in the 1860 census, certain patterns emerge (Table XVII). Most clearly, Know-Nothingism was in no sense a class movement. It cut through the native-born population much as that population appeared on the 1860 census rolls. There were differences, however, important not only in and of themselves, but because they tend to contradict recent interpretations of from what segments of society the Know-Nothings drew their strength. Writing in 1970, Seymour M.

Lipset and Earl Raab attempted to prove, with virtually no evidence, that Know-Nothingism was essentially a lower class Protestant movement, a movement of artisans and laborers with virtually no support among the country's elite.[8] Yet in Jersey City it was the skilled workers

TABLE XVII

COMPARISON BY OCCUPATION OF KNOW-NOTHINGS, 1856, WITH ALL NATIVE-BORN MALES, 20 AND OVER, 1860*

Occupation	KNOW-NOTHINGS, 1856		NATIVE-BORN, 1860	
	N	%	N	%
Economic elite	107	22.5	470	16.7
Professional	17	3.6	140	5.0
White collar	73	15.3	570	20.2
Shop-keepers	69	14.5	167	5.9
Artisan	110	23.1	728	25.8
Building trades	25	5.2	241	8.6
Unskilled	43	9.0	254	9.0
Government	16	3.4	47	1.7
No occupation	16	3.4	201	7.1
TOTAL	476	100.0%	2818	100.0%

who responded least well to Know-Nothing appeals. While skilled workers (artisans and men in the building trades) made up 34.4% of the native-born males in 1860, they constituted only 28.5% of the Know-Nothings in 1856. Members of the economic elite, however, were over-represented. Almost half again as many merchants, bankers, brokers, and manufacturers signed the Filmore and Donelson petition as their numbers in the community warranted.

---

*Occupational data on the Know-Nothings in 1856 is taken from the 1855 and 1856 Jersey City city directories. The 1860 data on all native-born males, twenty and over, is taken from the 1860 manuscript census (Table II, Chapter II).

Two other groups were also over-represented, groups which probably encountered lower class immigrants on a day-to-day basis more than most in the city: shop-keepers and policemen. While only 5.9% of the city's native-born men were shop-keepers in 1860, they made up 14.8% of the Know-Nothing vote in 1856. The proportion of policemen was also high. Of twenty men on the force in September 1856, six signed the petition, 31.6% of the whole.[9] Nativism, then, found its strongest support not in the city's artisan community but among the city's elite and among those who most regularly came into contact with the immigrant population.

Recent unpublished research, although impressionistic, tends to confirm these conclusions. Thomas J. Curran found that in New York State it was the "high rent urban districts" that most consistently voted Know-Nothing during the mid-1850's.[10] Writing on Connecticut, Richard D. Parmet found that the oldest families were heavily represented in the membership, and that of 248 Know-Nothing legislators elected in 1855, ninety-one were merchants, manufacturers or professionals. While almost half were farmers (an occupational category unrelated to social class) only sixteen were artisans. Here again Know-Nothingism would hardly appear to have been a largely working class phenomenon.[11]

While Know-Nothingism was primarily a native-born movement, it was not exclusively so. As Michael F. Holt and Ronald P. Formisano have demonstrated, the movement found strong support among British and Irish Protestants who brought a heritage of anti-Catholicism with them as immigrants. Jersey City's Know-Nothings were no exception. The four Negus brothers, for example, were British, and George D. Chapin was a Protestant Irish merchant. While the party elite seem to have been native-born, in Jersey City the support among immigrant Protestants argues strongly that the Know-Nothing movement was, as elsewhere, more specifically anti-Catholic than anti-foreign.[12] This was illustrated at the April 1856 Democratic nominating convention. Noting that many Democrats were members of nativistic societies "bitterly opposed to himself and his co-religionists," a Mr. Somers introduced a resolution obliging candidates to swear they were not members of any secret society. This resolution was later withdrawn in the face of vigorous opposition; significantly, in urging adoption Somers chose to dwell only on the religious aspects of nativism.[13]

Anti-Catholicism formed an essential part of American nationalism. Men who defined themselves largely in terms of their culture's Protestantism were, like Assemblyman Roberts, disturbed by Catholic attempts to enter into and change that culture. Know-Nothingism represented a desire to return to the basic Protestant hegemony that existed before the Irish immigration began.[14] A Jersey City Know-

Nothing newspaper made this point in 1859:

> Our creed is <u>American</u> suffrage, <u>American</u> Sabbaths and <u>American</u> legislation. We would strengthen "the things that remain" of our fathers against the arrogant insolence of German infidelity, against Irish mobocracy, and against the crafty cunning of a wily Jesuitical and foreign influence domination.[15]

Here the secular and the religious blended inseparably. To the evangelical Protestant the Sabbath and the ballot were almost equally sacred, and a major function of elected government was to preserve the evangelical conception of ordered freedom. Non-evangelical Germans and Irish Catholics both posed a threat to what many mid-nineteenth century Americans saw as traditional values.

While the Know-Nothing vote came from all segments of native-born society, the leadership came very clearly from the city's economic elite. At the Hudson County American convention in the fall of 1856 eleven of the twenty members were merchants or professionals. While few seem to have had much prior political experience, the majority of these men were politically active over the next twenty years. William Dunning, editor of the party's small weekly, was connected with various Republican newspapers from 1858 to his death in the 1870's, and John Lyons, head of the O. U. A. in New Jersey, published a nativistic Democratic daily from 1859 to 1875. Publisher of the city's annual directory, James Gopsill was elected mayor in 1867 by a coalition of Republicans and native-born Democrats. Two others served as police chiefs after 1860, one as recorder, and four as school board members. Most importantly, their actions showed that they retained their nativism after the demise of the Know-Nothing party. We shall see that through the 1860's and 1870's former Know-Nothings played a large role in both the Republican and Democratic parties.[16]

The American party captured 28.0% of the vote in Jersey City in 1856, a higher percentage than it received state-wide or nationally (see Table XVIII). As many voters were Irish Catholics and Germans, the percentage of native-born voters who supported Filmore and Donelson must have been much higher than 28.0%. In neighboring Bergen, for

TABLE XVIII

1856 PRESIDENTIAL ELECTION RETURNS
JERSEY CITY, NEW JERSEY, UNITED STATES

Party	JERSEY CITY N	%	NEW JERSEY N	%	UNITED STATES N	%
Republican	876	29.1	28368	28.8	1,339,932	33.1
Democratic	1291	42.9	46368	47.2	1,832,955	45.3
American	840	28.0	23604	24.0	871,731	21.6
TOTAL	3007	100.0%	98340	100.0%	4,044,618	100.0%

example, where native-born citizens predominated, Filmore received 56.3% of the vote. It would not be unreasonable to assume that Jersey City's native-born voters gave him a comparable percentage.[17] When the American State Council met in Newark after the election to analyze the result, they felt that the important issues had been obscured by "the whirlwind of passion and fanaticism which under the guise of 'bleeding Kansas' had swept over the North." Feeling that "in the late election, the line has been drawn with terrible distinction between the native and the foreign vote," they recommended re-organization to include "those who honestly believe in the great principle that 'Americans shall rule America.'"[18] While the American party was unsuccessful in forming a winning coalition that could concentrate on immigration and ignore slavery, the "great principle" of America for the Americans expressed itself in Jersey City in other ways.

III

The essential Protestantism of Jersey City nativism was best revealed in two organizations created in the early 1850's, the Hudson County Bible Society and its complement, the Jersey City City Mission and Tract Society. Part of a nation-wide response to Catholic immigration, they sought to protect Protestant society by bringing evangelical religion and middle class morality to those who brought neither to Jersey City. Formed in October 1852, the Hudson County Bible Society had as its goal placing a Protestant Bible in every Catholic home. During its first year, it employed hired and volunteer colporteurs to visit every family in Hudson County, selling or giving a Bible to every family "destitute" of the Scriptures. The first annual report sounded a note of urgency that very clearly tied the society's missionary endeavors to the political and cultural consequences of immigration. The "foreign element which is so rapidly flowing into this country," the report noted, "is destined, at no distant day, to exert an immense, if not controlling, influence in our county affairs, both political and religious."[19]

The Germans, the report continued, demanded "the most careful and earnest attention of this Society." Besides practicing a "cold formalism" and entertaining "loose and dangerous views of the Sabbath," they displayed a "<u>jealousy of all Christian institutions, especially the Christian ministry</u>," and cannot conceive of a clergyman, except as a wolf in sheep's clothing, whose only purpose is to . . . reduce them to vassalage." One German told a German colporteur, "It was the strangest thing he ever saw, that a German was going about among his countrymen in this free land, trying to bring them again under the yoke of priests and tyrants. It was a shame for Germany." In terms of numbers, "about a third are avowedly infidels, and another third are professedly Catholics, but are really skeptics in that peculiar transition state through which so many pass from the superstitions of Romanism to the blankest infidelity. This infidelity is not latent, but active."[20]

While the Germans exhibited "<u>gross infidelity</u>," the Irish were "slaves of Papal intolerance," and would not accept Protestant Bibles. Confident of victory if placed on equal terms, the Society demanded, "Let the Romish priests remove the ban which they have placed upon the American Bible Society, and leave out its publications from their list of forbidden books, and we shall see who is responsible for all this ignorance and superstition."[21]

A year later, in 1853, Alderman Justus Slater, chairman of the Committee on Alms, sought to raise support for sustained Protestant preaching to the largely Irish inmates in the Alms House. From this spark, the Protestant community organized the Jersey City City Mission and Tract Society, modeled on a similar organization in New York City, with a board of managers containing representatives from each Protestant church.[22] "The object of this society," read the constitution, "shall be to provide spiritual instruction for those who are destitute of the means of grace,--the general periodical circulation of religious Tracts, and the temporal relief for the poor in Jersey City."[23] For the next twenty-nine years the society worked at these twin goals in the order stated; temporal relief never got in the way of tract distribution. Like the Bible Society, the City Mission and Tract Society was a religious organization whose goals had obvious political implications. The poor of Jersey City were the Irish of Jersey City, and the Irish, as an American Tract Society pamphlet noted, "are crowding our cities, lining our railroads and canals, occupying our kitchens, driving our carriages, and <u>electing our rulers</u>. They are priest-ridden and deluded, and, what is worse, love to have it so." But if "a pure Gospel, with its restraining, elevating power" could be brought to them, "we have nothing to fear for our civil institutions."[24] The religious and the secular blended in a view of society that held religious institutions to be the foundations of civil order, and evangelicalism to be in many ways synonymous with Americanism. Jersey City's immigrants, thought the Hudson County Bible Society, "urgently need the teachings of divine truth."[25]

Immediately after organizing, in November 1853, the City Mission and Tract Society sought a full-time paid missionary. Five months later, in April 1854, they hired one of the city's clergy, the Rev. William G. Verrinder of the small Union Baptist Church. Born in England in 1805 to Episcopalian parents, he married and immigrated in 1832 and worked as a compositor in Buffalo and Cincinnati before ordination as a Baptist minister. He had churches in western New York and Providence, Rhode Island, before coming to Jersey City in 1849, where he not only preached, but was active in temperance work.[26] Beginning as missionary in April 1854, in one month he divided this city of 20,000 into 157 districts, and assigned seventy-eight "tract visitors" to ninety-eight different districts. The society distributed 2813 tracts to 3046 families. By December these figures had doubled, and of 5899 families visited, 5636 accepted tracts, with the net result that two people were induced to attend church.[27]

Verrinder, as City Missionary, occupied a quasi-official position in Jersey City. From the inception of the society in 1854 to his retirement in 1882, he preached and counseled in the Alms House and prison every Sunday and attended the annual examinations in the public schools with the school board. Through his monthly and annual reports, printed with steady regularity by the city's press, he recommended measures to deal with the poor, the disorderly, and the irreligious. The society worked not only to change beliefs and behavior, but also to monitor the conditions and problems among the poor, and especially the Catholic poor of Jersey City.

In dealing with the poor, Verrinder offered suggestions heavy with discipline and control. As he believed the root of poverty to be intemperance, he repeatedly urged prohibitory legislation. If strictly enforced, he wrote in 1870, "there would be, comparatively, very little crime and pauperism in our city." Accepting the concept of an open, mobile society, he found temperance "the steppingstone to everything that is honorable and upright; and not infrequently does it conduct to competence and even wealth." In Verrinder's view, society did indeed bear a limited responsibility for poverty and destitution in Jersey City; but this responsibility lay only in its failure to control liquor, thereby allowing "drunkenness, and its attendant evils of poverty, disease and crime."[28] Never did he suggest that poverty was other than the result of individual failure; society erred only by allowing men unnecessary temptation. The amount of money expended on "temporal relief" reflected this view, and was always small. While receiving a salary that averaged $1500 a year, Verrinder dispersed during twenty years $10,475.99--an average of $523.80 a year. During the 1857 depression Verrinder vigorously defended his policy of distributing tracts to the poor rather than food, claiming spiritual aid was more beneficial in the long run. The editor of the Telegraph, however, thought the policy "to be the offspring of a disordered brain--a perfect negation . . . that looks almost like laughing at a portion of our race."[29] The young also received Verrinder's attention. Repeatedly urging the establishment of "ragged" schools and reformatories, he sought to rid the city of "scores of children" developing "idle and vicious habits" on the streets. Mandatory school attendance, he felt, would prevent children from begging for their parents, and assist in "cultivating habits of thrift and industry." The school's role, he held, was the transmission of middle class values to lower class youths, with attendance exacted by force where it was not forthcoming by persuasion.[30]

Verrinder never lost sight of the society's primary purpose, "to win souls to Christ," and his primary weapons here were the tracts of the American Tract Society. Working with the tract visitors, mostly women from the city's evangelical churches, Verrinder canvassed the city monthly. The results for February 1860 were typical (Table XIX).[31]

TABLE XIX

CITY MISSIONARY'S REPORT, FEBRUARY, 1860

Families visited	7,095
Tracts distributed	7,331
Declined	335
Bibles supplied	9
Testaments to children	3
Induced to attend Sunday School	22
Induced to attend public school	3
Promised to attend church	4
Backsliders reclaimed	1
Hopeful conversions	1
Cases of inquiry	3

Excerpts from the visitors' reports occasionally appeared in the press, and these talked of infidelity and Catholicism, not poverty. One visitor reported talking to a man "who plainly told him that he had no Bible in the house, that he did not want one, that the Priest was his guide, that it was his intercession on which he relied. The visitor hopes yet to benefit this man by conversing with him."[32] A young woman commented, "A number of R. C. families reside in my district, and though often rough words greet me, and doors are closed against me in their homes, the glad welcome of some humble follower of Jesus is sure to meet me in another."[33] Another, conscious of ethnic differences, wrote, "I find some interesting colored families who are very thankful for the tracts; and also several German families, all of whom receive the tracts cheerfully. Among the Irish I met with sixteen refusals."[34] Infidelity also received comment. Entering a store run by an Irishman, Verrinder reported an unexpected reply to his greeting:

> "Paine's works are my Scriptures." He seemed a well informed man, and a customer, who came into the shop while he was making the remark, said, "You mean the Age of Reason, don't you? That's my Bible too." It was in vain that the missionary expostulated. They only laughed at him.[35]

A Bible Society colporteur reported occasional meetings "with those who advocated infidel sentiments; sometimes even women expressing the gloomy belief that death is an everlasting sleep."[36]

Catholic response was not encouraging. They saw the tract and Bible societies for what they were--active agents of Protestant proselytism. The reports of the tract visitors and the relative unimportance of "temporal relief" in the activities of the City Mission and Tract Society made this plain. The Catholic community, however, displayed its hostility in silence. Catholics consistently refused Bibles offered by the Bible Society. In 1856, a Hudson City colporteur found 39 families destitute, of whom 38 refused to accept Protestant Bibles. In 1869 all 50 destitute Protestant families in Jersey City accepted Bibles, but only 18 of 1322 destitute Catholic families accepted, less than two percent.[37] Although criticism of the societies seldom reached the press, after the <u>American Standard</u> printed Verrinder's 1864 Bible Society report, in which he referred to the Catholic population as "exceedingly ignorant, superstitious and bigoted," the editor received a trenchant letter from "H." "H." noted that Verrinder's salary, equal to that of four Catholic priests, was received "for doing nothing or next to nothing, but bore and disgust the majority of the poor." He then asked,

> What does the City Missionary do for his $1500 per annum? Oh, like a good pharasee he parades his great works, his sermons (bless the mark), and the number of times he said prayers! Amazing apostle! worthy imitator of St. Paul! With what arithmetical skill he sums up the 777 visits (mystic numbers) and the 214 sermons (God help the hearers) and the number of <u>promised</u> to go to church! what a matter of figures of dollars and cents is this City Missionaryship! But of course the <u>pious</u> laity who support the Tract Society, must see something done by their well-paid functionary, whose $1500 a year comes from their generous pockets.
> The "<u>ignorant</u>, <u>bigoted</u>, and <u>superstitious</u> Roman Catholics do not contribute to his salary, and hence the modern city apostle turns up his eyes in pious horror, like a duck in a thunderstorm and calls them hard names and boasts about the Bible and displays his Biblical lore for the edification of the innocent victims of the tract society.

"H." offered to pit any sixteen-year-old Catholic boy against Verrinder in a test of Bible lore, with any two ministers and one priest as judges. He received no reply.[38]

The Bible and tract societies also had close ties with the city's school system. It is no exaggeration to view the schools as an extension of the Protestant community. The city's first school board, appointed by the aldermen when they gave up direct control of the schools in 1852, contained twelve men. Five of them held office in either the Bible or tract society before 1860, and three others became Know-Nothings by 1856. The board that took office in 1857 was much the same. It contained four men who were or had been managers of one society or the other, the 1853 alderman who had originally suggested the City Mission and Tract Society, the superintendent of the Temperance Sabbath School, and three Know-Nothings.[39] Although no managers of the societies were elected aldermen, the aldermen consistently appointed men identified with evangelism and nativism to the school board. No Catholic served on the school board until 1865 when the aldermen appointed Harold Henwood, a native-born convert. Similarly, every superintendent of schools before 1870 was identified with one of these two societies. Abram S. Jewell, for example, the superintendent in 1857, was also treasurer of the Bible Society. Although an elective office, the superintendency was seldom contested; both parties, probably by pre-arrangement, usually nominated the same man.[40]

Not surprisingly, very few Catholic children attended the public schools in the 1850's, and by 1854 St. Peter's school enrolled 600 students. In 1857 Jersey City Catholics, in conjunction with Newark Catholics, circulated petitions against the school system, seeking state relief from taxation for "sectarian" schools. Bishop James Roosevelt Bayley, who thought the union of "School & State . . . a greater injustice than [a union of] Church & State," squelched the petition, however, as detrimental to long-run Catholic interests.[41] Catholics also objected to Verrinder's suggestion of a "ragged" school on the grounds that "it would only serve to engender strifes and dissensions . . . here, as it has done in England."[42]

The Bible and tract societies aimed, as did the Know-Nothing party, at preserving America as an evangelical Protestant country. One worked to limit immigration, the other to change the beliefs of those already arrived. The religious societies were fully aware of the possible political consequences of "great cities swarming with churchless, Christless Europeans."[43] The city missionary constantly urged prohibitory legislation rigorously enforced by the police, and "ragged" schools and reformatories in which to incarcerate the young. Closely tied to Jersey City's municipal government, the societies drew their strength from the self-conscious Protestantism of the city's native-born as a large community of lower class Catholics settled in·their midst.

IV

The City Missionary's quasi-official position became a source of contention in August 1857 when Catholics petitioned the aldermen, complaining that Catholic paupers in the Alms House were subject to religious coercion. The controversy revealed not only the essentially Protestant and proselytizing nature of the city's institutions, but also Catholic response, a response which usually received little attention in the city's press. The petition, signed by Henry Beirne, an Irish store-keeper, and twenty-three others, charged that their "co-religionists" were forced to attend Verrinder's weekly service where he "revile[d] the religious faith of those who are compelled to hear him." Complaining that children were especial objects of Protestant proselytism, they urged that children be given only books and instruction that conformed with the religious beliefs of the parents. Adult paupers, they recommended, should have the opportunity to attend nearby St. Peter's "under such regulations as may prevent abuse of the privilege." The aldermen referred the petition to the committee on alms.[44]

Opened in March 1852, the Alms House was in its fifth

year of operation and had been under the continuous supervision of William Whitley, a sixty-seven-year-old native-born Protestant. The paupers, on the other hand, were Irish and Catholic. The 1860 census counted 44 adult paupers of whom 34 were Irish. The 42 children in the institution were largely native-born, but with distinctly Irish names. Religious instruction had begun late in 1853 when Alderman Justus Slater requested regular preaching from the Protestant clergy. Verrinder had preached regularly since May 1854, and a group of Protestant women began a Sunday School soon after.[45] Thanking Whitley and his wife in his 1856 annual report, Verrinder wrote, "They have, both by their presence and in various ways, encouraged the attendance of those in their charge."[46]

In 1857 the Board of Aldermen's committee of alms consisted of three men. Matthew Erwin and Robert B. Kashow were both native-born anti-Catholics,[*] and Robert Cornelison was Irish. The committee heard testimony from twenty-three inmates and former inmates, and on September 15, a month after the submission of the petition, issued its reports. Erwin and Kashow signed a majority report that found the charges "ill founded and groundless," and "purely imaginary." Religious instruction consisted only of "doctrine or principles . . . held in common by all denom-

---

[*]See page 52.

inations of christians." They advised no changes in Alms House administration.[47] Cornelison wrote his own report, claiming that the majority report was written, signed and submitted without consulting him, that Kashow was often absent from the committee's sessions, and that Erwin called the allegations "false and groundless" before hearing any testimony and would have no notes taken. Twelve witnesses, Cornelison wrote, testified "that Catholic paupers were threatened for non-attendance at preaching and worship in the Alms House; and that they labored under the impression that such attendance was the rule of the institution." Citing instances of children abused for non-attendance, he held that special pressures were put on youthful inmates. He recommended the end of all coercion in religious matters, and that the aldermen hear complaints at the Alms House once a month. "These memorialists," he reminded his audience, "represent a class of our citizens who . . . own more than a million of dollars worth of property in our city, and they pay their share of taxes, and have therefore a deep interest in the welfare of our Institutions."[48]

Meanwhile, a different aspect of the controversy developed away from the aldermanic chambers. James M. Brann, director of the school attached to St. Peter's, published a letter in the <u>Daily Sentinel</u> requesting that the Rev. John Kelly preach at the Alms House to the Catholic inmates. Born in Ireland in 1805, Kelly emigrated in 1825, was ordained in 1833, and spent three years working as a missionary in Liberia before assuming the Pastorate of St. Peter's in 1844. Vigorous in his defense of the city's Irish, he once blamed the bad press the Irish received on editors who accepted British money.[49] While the aldermen studied Henry Beirne's petition, Kelly responded to Brann's letter, and went to the Alms House on three successive Sundays to preach to the Catholic inmates. Arriving at the scheduled worship hour, 2 p. m., he found Verrinder ready to preach his usual service on each occasion. Verrinder did not object to Kelly's presence or to his conducting a service. But Verrinder objected strongly to Kelly's holding a <u>sectarian</u> service that was intended for Catholics only. Kelly must either preach to all inmates, as would any Protestant exchange minister, or not preach at all. Kelly withdrew each time. Verrinder then defended his behavior in the press by citing the "unsectarian" nature of his own services.[50]

Kelly was not through. Writing to the <u>Sentinel</u>, he admitted that since the aldermen began investigating the Alms House, religious coercion of adults had largely ceased, "but the juvenile Catholic paupers are <u>still obliged</u> <u>to</u> <u>attend</u> this established (?) worship, and this, undoubtedly, after all, is religious coercion and at the same time systematic proselytism." He had been denied a separate service, he claimed, "because of prejudice and the job of proselytizing Catholic children."[51] Verrinder replied that he had given Kelly the opportunity to conduct an unsectarian service, but he had not accepted. If he wanted to hold a sectarian service he would have to do so at some other time than Sunday afternoon. Verrinder suggested that Kelly had attempted to get Catholics to boycott his services, but, he claimed, "the intelligent Catholic inmates" attended anyway.[52]

The aldermen promulgated new rules for the Alms House in December. While forbidding religious coercion of adults, the rules required children "to attend divine service and Sabbath School once on every Sabbath day of such denomination as they or any of them may prefer." As they could not leave the institution without explicit permission, and as no "sectarian" preaching was allowed in the Alms House, it is unclear what this changed. Adult paupers, while not required to attend services, were required to remain in their rooms during the scheduled worship hours if they chose not to attend. The Catholic petition, then, gained the paupers little. Adults could remain in their rooms, and children could hear whom they pleased, providing he was not a "sectarian." Verrinder remained within the Alms House and Kelly without, a situation ratified by Aldermen Erwin and Kashow, who upheld Verrinder in preventing "the spectacle of the introduction of sectarianism into an institution."[53] When the voters defeated Erwin for state assemblyman later that fall, by a margin of ten votes, the Catholic New York Tablet found it a subject worthy of comment.[54]

Jersey City's press firmly supported the Protestant position and gave Catholic charges no credence and little sympathy. A spokesman for Jersey City's Irish, however, was Bernard D. Killian, a fourth ward resident and editor of the Tablet. In 1858 Killian charged the aldermen with profiting from Alms House contracts, a charge not taken up by the Jersey City press. When Killian left for the west in May 1858, the Young Men's Catholic Institute of Jersey City presented him with a gold watch and resolutions praising his "public spirited course here, as evinced by his writings on behalf of even-handed justice to the poor of Jersey City."[55]

V

The Alms House controversy revealed the tie between the city's elite and evangelical Protestantism. Two years later labor troubles among workers on the Erie Railroad's tunnel through Bergen Hill demonstrated the class nature of Jersey City nativism in other ways. In 1856 the Erie began to tunnel through the lower end of the Palisades, called Bergen Hill in Jersey City, to connect their small Hudson River terminal with their tracks in the low-lying swampland behind the hill. Although the Erie's main line ran through New York from Dunkirk on Lake Erie to Piermont, seventeen miles north of Manhattan on the Hudson, the company had transferred its passenger business to Jersey City in the early 1850's, using the Paterson and Hudson Railroad's tracks. The tunnel, coupled with great expansion along the waterfront, including the building of the 1000-foot "Long Dock" into the Hudson (using tunnel rubble), would allow the railroad to transfer more of its operations to a site directly opposite Manhattan. By 1862, two years after completion, the company felt that its Jersey City facilities saved it $100,000 a month in re-handling costs over the Piermont site.[56]

The tunnel, built by sinking shafts every five hundred feet, and working in both directions from these, required large numbers of unskilled laborers, who created a shanty village over and around the tunnel. As Jersey City ended at the base of the hill, most of this activity took place in neighboring Hudson City. But Jersey Cityites watched with trepidation as over a thousand unskilled Irish laborers built their shacks and went to work almost in their midst. Hudson City residents were no less displeased. The tunnel progressed in fits and starts as Erie finances allowed, and when unemployed, the workers were considered a social menace. During the winter of 1857 a Jersey City paper reported vigilante committees "a l'California" to drive them out, and in 1858, when the city put men whose families were "in a starving condition" to work breaking paving stones, a letter in the Telegraph advised running them out instead. The Hudson County Democrat, in 1864, saw Hudson's progress "kept back by the lawless population introduced during the building of the wonderful Erie Tunnel."[57]

The tunnel workers organized their community along Irish regional lines. When Munster men and Connought men, for example, clashed in 1857 over land for enlarging their respective villages atop Bergen Hill, the sheriff called out the militia to suppress the minor violence. Later that year, when the contractor failed to raise money for the semi-monthly payroll paid in store orders, the sheriff again called out the militia--at the railroad's request--in case of violence, although none materialized.[58] The workers struggled through the next two years with periods of unemployment and partial employment as the Erie experienced bankruptcy and receivership and the tunnel a new contractor. Then, on Friday, September 16, 1859, contractor Alfred B. Seymour announced that wages due on the 15th, for August's work--and to be paid in store orders--would not be forthcoming until early October. The men stopped work immediately.[59]

The trains also stopped. The men moved from the tunnel to the Erie tracks that snaked around the hill, and barricaded them with a pile of old wagons, lumber and dirt, preventing Erie trains from entering or leaving Jersey City. The barricade remained through the night, guarded by from three to seven hundred men who sat in a drenching rain roasting corn and potatoes and singing to the music of two violins and a flute. "Hell alive with bonfires," one reporter called it. On Saturday morning railroad officials, anxious for militia protection, sought Sheriff Henry B. Beatty, but he was nowhere to be found. Having never been reimbursed when he called out the militia in 1857, Beatty "kept out of the way" and spent a pleasant day at the state fair. Meanwhile, the Hudson City Mayor and Father Aloysius Vanuta of Hudson City's St. Joseph's Church talked to the men, advising them to give up their position while others tried to get them their money. The sheriff, when he returned, likewise addressed them, as did militia general James T. Hatfield, who told them that if they persisted they would be shot. Hatfield called out two militia regiments, including an artillery unit that arrived with four field pieces but no ammunition. While the laborers weathered another night in the rain, the militia slept in the courthouse, waiting for daylight before assaulting the barricade.[60]

What transpired on Sunday illustrated both the fears

of native-born citizens and the essentially non-violent nature of the demonstration. The militia marched to the tracks below the barricade and boarded a flat car that was pushed by a locomotive toward the barricade. Father Vanuta and Mayor Collard addressed the men again, and Collard finally read the riot act. A curious dialogue followed:

> One of them remarked, "This is no riot; we want our money."
> Mayor Collard--"It looks very much like a riot."
> Another man said, "We want our money that we've worked this two months hard for, and we have a right to it."
> Another of the tunnel men said, "We endanger our lives every day for a dollar or nine shillings. Now if we cannot get our money for this, to get food for our wives and children, we may as well die as not."

Then, as laborers left the railroad cars to remove the barricade, strikers rolled stones and steel "frogs" onto the track before and behind the military train. A few threw stones at the militiamen, but "many of the rioters denounced this act." The militia disembarked and the crowd retreated. As an estimated five thousand spectators lined the hills around the point of confrontation, the militia went through the crowd and without resistance arrested about forty "ring-leaders." Bound, tied together and thrown into a baggage car, these men were later hauled to the county jail. The crowd dispersed, the barricade was dismantled, and the trains rolled. The militia regrouped and then marched to the laborers' village, where they systematically searched every shanty for men who had engaged in the riot. Men were pulled from under beds and chased across fields. Another thirty were thus arrested, and after one arrest in which the subject was badly beaten, the women "cursed their lords for not having courage to effect a rescue."[61]

Seventy-three men were arrested and brought to the county jail. Only one, the New York Herald reported, was armed, and he with a set of brass knuckles. Many were said to be mere boys. "Among the most unruly of the crowd," reported the Herald, were John McCabe and his older brother Patrick, aged twelve. They too spent most of a day bound in a baggage car and a night in jail. On the following day the families of those arrested gathered outside the jail seeking information and relief. "One woman, who was in a very delicate condition, declared she had nothing in the house for herself or her children to eat, and they must either let her husband out or take the rest of the family in."[62] The examination of the prisoners began the next day. Each prisoner was brought into court and members of the militia or Jersey City police force attempted to identify each one. When Michael Andre was identified and asked if he wished to reply to his accusers, he replied, "What's the use of a fellow bothering himself? They will swear to anything." He was bound over for the Grand Jury, as was Michael Mulvey, heard to shout when the militia charged, "Come on, boys, every one take his man, and we shall clear every son of a b---h of them."[63] Thirty-three--including the two McCabe boys--were bound over for the Grand Jury with bail set at $500 for most, at least two years' wages for any of these men. Two weeks later the Grand Jury indicted six of them, and in trials a month later that attracted little attention, six were convicted of riot, and of obstructing the tracks. They were all sentenced to two years in jail on each count, the sentences to run concurrently.[64]

The Jersey City American Standard saw the "TERRIBLE RIOT OF THE TUNNEL MEN" as one more indication that the question "Who is to rule America?" was being answered the wrong way. When wages were not paid on time, the editor felt, "American employees wait patiently . . . but these imported beggars take the law into their own hands."

> All this is tolerated, aye and encouraged too by designing politicians, because these animals may be used with benefit at the polls, and next November every one of them, not in durance vile, having sworn "to support the constitution of the United States and that of New Jersey"!! without knowing one syllable of what is contained in either, will be marched up to "the ballot box, the Palladium of American liberty," and there deposit his precious vote for his friend and patron, the Democratic nominee. So much for un-

> kenneling this mongrel mass of ignorance and
> crime and superstition, as utterly unfit for
> its duties, as they are for the common cour-
> tesies and decencies of civilized life.[65]

The poverty of the tunnel men elicited sympathy, however, as well as fear. In Hoboken a group of citizens met, and while upholding the course pursued by Hudson City's Mayor Collard, voted to begin a collection to relieve the acute distress engendered by non-payment of wages. A correspondent to the Courier and Advertiser felt that the "question for law and order citizens to consider" was railroad behavior in not paying their men. The workers, he claimed, "feel that they have earned their money and should have it, and the public says so too."[66]

In retrospect the tunnel riot was a minor disturbance. Strikers held a barricade for two rainy nights and were then dispersed without bloodshed. The only casualties were two policemen who were hit with stones, neither of whom required medical attention. The significance of the riot lay in the fact that Irish laborers turned to extralegal means to achieve what they perceived as just ends. As Jersey City had not previously experienced this type of group behavior and as it clearly violated middle class behavioral norms, Jersey City's elite responded in ways that demonstrated the social cleavage in the community. While the rioters huddled around their fires singing to the music of a wet flute, rumors circulated through Jersey City that the men were preparing to sack the city.[67] As years passed, the violence of the riot grew in the popular memory, at least of the native-born, to coincide with the perceived threat at the time. When Father Vanuta died in 1876, his obituary in the local Republican paper stressed how he "had done more than an entire police force could have done in quelling riotous assemblages and driving to their homes drunken and unruly men."[68] By 1895, when Alexander McLean wrote his History of Jersey City, the barricade of over-turned wagons and dirt had become "a wall built of rocks and mortar," and when the troops attempted to remove it, they "moved slowly under a shower of stones and insults from the brutal mob."[69] While some of the city's elite may have sympathized with the tunnel men and agreed with the New York Herald reporter who wrote, "The tunnel men are very poor, and . . . have been greatly oppressed," more seem to have agreed with John Lyons, editor of the American Standard, and a former Know-Nothing, that "these animals" were "a mongrel mass of ignorance and crime and superstition."[70]

The tunnel strike, and the response to it, illustrated how the Protestant elite responded to the Irish as unskilled laborers, poorer than any other group in Jersey City. Although their only objective was the payment of wages due them, by seeking it through direct action they called forth a host of irrelevant but very real fears on the part of many native-born citizens who feared a lower class alien presence. Ethnic relations in Jersey City suffered from class as well as religious antagonism. When Irishmen began to enter politics in numbers after 1860, the first aspect of the city's administration that they consciously sought to control was the administration of justice. Not surprisingly, they met vigorous resistance.

DOCUMENTATION: CHAPTER III

[1] *Daily Sentinel and Advertiser*, April 4, 1854 (hereafter cited as *Sentinel*).

[2] The 1850 figure includes the population of Jersey City (6856) and the population of Van Vorst township (4617), which merged into Jersey City in 1851. State of New Jersey, Department of State, Census Bureau, *Compendium of Censuses 1726-1905, Together with the Tabulated Returns of 1905* (Trenton, 1906), p. 24.

[3] *Hudson County Courier*, May 7 through July 16, 1857.

[4] Ibid., July 16, 1857.

[5] Ibid., May 7 and 21, 1857.

[6] *American Standard*, March 29, 1861 (hereafter cited as *Standard*).

[7] *Hudson County Courier*, September 4, 1856. I have been unable to find any comparable information on the membership of the various secret societies in the city.

[8] Seymour M. Lipset and Earl Raab, *The Politics of Unreason: Right Wing Extremism in America, 1790-1970* (New York, 1970), pp. 54-58.

[9] *Daily Telegraph*, September 17, 1856 (hereafter cited as *Telegraph*).

[10] Thomas J. Curran, "The Know Nothings in New York" (Ph.D. Dissertation, Columbia, 1963), p. 306.

[11] Robert D. Parmet, "The Know-Nothings in Connecticut" (Ph.D. Dissertation, Columbia, 1966), pp. 151-158. Leon C. Soule argues that in New Orleans the Know-Nothing party, dominant from 1854 to 1862, split along class lines with an "aristocratic" and a "workingmen's" faction. Before 1858, however, it was dominated by members of the native-born Protestant elite and even contained some Catholic Creoles. The movement, however, did not originate in the working classes. *The Know Nothing Party in New Orleans: A Reappraisal* (Baton Rouge, 1961), pp. 65-67, 85-117.

[12] Michael F. Holt, *Forging a Majority: The Formation of the Republican Party in Pittsburgh, 1848-1860* (New Haven,

1969), pp. 123-174; Ronald P. Formisano, *The Birth of Mass Political Parties, Michigan, 1827-1861* (Princeton, 1971), pp. 247-253.

[13] *Telegraph*, April 1, 1856.

[14] Billington, pp. 262-280.

[15] *Standard*, September 22, 1859.

[16] *Telegraph*, October 6, 1856.

[17] Ibid., November 5, 1856. For the role of the Know-Nothings in state politics, see Charles M. Knapp, *New Jersey Politics During the Civil War and Reconstruction* (Geneva, 1924), pp. 13-23.

[18] *Sentinel*, December 12, 1856.

[19] *First Annual Report of the Hudson County Bible Society, 1853* (New York, 1853), p. 7.

[20] Ibid., p. 3.

[21] Ibid., p. 9.

[22] *Sentinel*, September 6, 1853. For New York, see Carroll S. Rosenberg, *Religion and the Rise of the American City: The New York Mission Movement, 1812-1870* (Ithaca, 1971), pp. 187-203.

[23] *Standard*, December 15, 1870.

[24] American Tract Society, *General Views of Colporteurage* (n.p., n.d.), pp. 31, 45. Internal evidence indicates that this was written in the early 1850's.

[25] *Standard*, November 3, 1860.

[26] *Sentinel*, December 8, 1849, September 3, 1853; *Journal*, October 16, 1891. In 1853 Verrinder was chairman of the Jersey City Temperance Society, a branch of the American Temperance Union.

[27] *Telegraph*, May 6, December 5, 1854. In neighboring Hoboken, twenty visitors distributed 11,000 tracts in English, German and French. *Sentinel*, April 4, 1854.

[28] *Journal*, June 13, 1870; *Standard*, December 15, 1873. On concepts of mobility in mid-century America, see

Stephen Thernstrom, Poverty and Progress: Social Mobility in a Nineteenth Century City (Atheneum ed., New York, 1969), pp. 56-79.

[29] During its first twenty years the society distributed 484,404 tracts. Standard, December 15, 1873.

[30] Telegraph, September 19, 1856; Courier and Advertiser, December 12, 1859; Jersey City Times, December 11, 1865; Standard, December 15, 1873.

[31] Standard, March 10, 1873.

[32] Courier and Advertiser, February 5, 1862.

[33] Ibid., July 6, 1860.

[34] Standard, February 27, 1861.

[35] Verrinder, p. 12.

[36] Standard, December 8, 1864.

[37] Fourth Annual Report of the Hudson County Bible Society, 1856 (Jersey City, 1857), p. 3; Jersey City Times, November 5, 1869.

[38] Standard, December 13, 1864.

[39] McLean, pp. 145-147.

[40] Ibid.

[41] American Celt (n.d.), quoted in Telegraph, April 5, 1854; Sister M. Hildegarde Yeager, The Life of James Roosevelt Bayley (Washington, 1947), pp. 161, 242.

[42] Manual of the Common Council of Jersey City, 1857-1858 (Jersey City, 1858, p. 62 (hereafter cited as Manual ... 1857-1858).

[43] Home Evangelization: A View of the Wants and Prospects of the Country, Based on the Facts and Relations of Colportage (n.p., n.d.), p. 24.

[44] Manual ... 1857-1858, p. 62. For a brief summary of the controversy, see John Gilmore Shea, A History of the Catholic Church within the Limits of the United States, Vol. IV (New York, 1892), pp. 505-506.

[45] Manual . . . 1857-1858, p. 61.

[46] Telegraph, January 14, 1856.

[47] Manual . . . 1857-1858, pp. 61-62.

[48] Ibid., pp. 62-63.

[49] John Francis Gough, St. Mary's in Jersey City: A History of the Parish, 1859-1938 (New York, 1938), p. 12; Sentinel, July 21, 1854.

[50] Sentinel, July 10, 16, and 28, 1857.

[51] Ibid., September 26, 1857.

[52] Ibid., September 28, 1857; Telegraph, October 1, 1857.

[53] Manual . . . 1857-1858, pp. 61-62, 88-92.

[54] Noted in Courier and Advertiser, November 11, 1857.

[55] Ibid., January 20, 1858; Telegraph, May 7, 1858.

[56] Reports of the President and Superintendent of the New York and Erie Railroad for the Year Ending September 30, 1855 (New York, 1855), pp. 12-15; A Statement of the Operation of the New York and Erie Railroad Under the Receivership from August 16, 1859, to December 31, 1861 (New York, 1862), pp. 12-14.

[57] Courier and Advertiser, November 23, 1857; Telegraph, March 8 and 15, 1858; Hudson County Democrat (Hoboken), December 16, 1864.

[58] Hudson County Courier, February 19, 1857; New York Tribune, September 16, 1857; Telegraph, October 10, 1857.

[59] Courier and Advertiser, September 17, 1859.

[60] Ibid.; New York Tribune, September 17, 1859; New York Herald, September 18, 1859.

[61] New York Herald, September 19, 1859.

[62] New York Times, September 21, 1859.

[63] Courier and Advertiser, September 20, 1859; New York Herald, September 21, 1859.

[64] *Courier and Advertiser*, October 25, 1859; *Newark Daily Advertiser*, October 24, November 1, 1859.

[65] *Standard*, September 20, 1859. The editor also noted that the riot contributed to "the demoralization of a Sabbath."

[66] *New York Herald*, September 19, 1859; *Courier and Advertiser*, September 23, 1859.

[67] *Courier and Advertiser*, September 19, 1859.

[68] *Journal*, January 24, 1876.

[69] McLean, p. 70.

[70] *New York Herald*, September 18, 1859; *Standard*, September 20, 1859.

CHAPTER IV

POLICE, COURTS, AND THE IRISH

1860 - 1868

Between 1860 and 1868 Jersey City became much less officially Protestant. The Irish gradually entered politics and began to force changes in city administration. Concentrating first on the processes of justice, the Irish bolted the Democratic party in 1861 and nominated and elected a lower class Englishman as City Recorder, a judicial position whose duties included the disposition of minor offenses such as public drunkenness. In 1862 they forced the Democratic nomination and the election of an Irish police chief, and by 1866 dominated the police force. The number of Irish on the Common Council also increased, although their influence was not equal to their numbers. However, the native-born elite did not allow this challenge to pass unheeded. They gerrymandered the city to limit Irish influence, kept a fairly firm grasp on the machinery of both parties, and in 1866 turned to the state legislature for a state-appointed police commission that dismissed Irishmen from the force and rigidly enforced the temperance laws. Yet Jersey City's immigrants could not be ignored in 1868 as they had been in 1857.

Throughout this period, nativism and anti-Catholicism continued to play a major role in local politics. Although the American party maintained its distinctiveness in New Jersey longer than in many other states, it began to splinter after 1859 as its adherents entered either the Republican or Democratic party. As the parties emerged from a period of flux, the Republican party was clearly Protestant, embracing native-born, German, British, and Protestant Irish voters. The Democratic party had the support of the city's Irish Catholics, but native-born Democrats, a distinct minority, controlled the party and held the important offices. The men who emerged as Democratic leaders by 1863 were largely former Know-Nothings who retained their nativism although it could only be expressed in subtle ways. As the Democratic party dominated the city throughout the 1860's, this cleavage was of great importance. Anti-Catholicism continued to be as important during the 1860's as it was during the 1850's. Although the party of the Irish ran the city, the Irish played a minor role in that party except on election day when they were expected to vote at least once. The American Standard, published by John Lyons, a former butcher and president of the State Council of the American Party in 1856, became the native-born Democrats' organ, and Lyons played a major role in keeping the city government a native-born preserve. Although a Democrat by 1861, Lyons founded the paper in 1859 to revive the local American party, which, he wrote, stood between the Democrats with their "hordes of voters fresh from the arena of European politics," and anti-slavery, "the hydra-headed monster" which "vomits forth its venom, destructive alike of the principles it <u>professes</u> to advocate and the Union it <u>professes</u> to honor and serve."[1] But as the American party continued to deteriorate, many left it for either the Republicans or the Democrats. The <u>Courier and Advertiser</u> commented pointedly on an 1860 local election:

> The scenes around the polls presented some exceedingly suggestive combinations. Among them we could not avoid admiring the facility with which the fraternization was effected between rampant Third Degree Know-Nothings and Roman Catholic Irishmen, and leading teetotallers of the prohibitory law school with the keepers of low, unlicensed groggeries.[2]

The Republican party also had its share of Know-Nothings. William B. Dunning published the Republican <u>Courier and Advertiser</u>, successor to his Know-Nothing <u>Hudson County Courier</u>, and the only Republican mayor during the decade was also a Know-Nothing. When the 1860 Republican State convention, under the leadership of two Know-Nothings, Ephraim Marsh of Jersey City and Governor William A. Newell, refused to pass resolutions favoring a longer naturalization period, the <u>Standard</u> fumed that this was an unwarranted attempt at wooing the German vote, "an element which is impregnated with infidelity, which is the enemy of our Holy Sabbath and our Public schools, and seeks the subversion of both."[3] By 1860, then, both Republicans and Democrats sought allies in the immigrant communities, and nativist sentiments were to some extent overcome but hardly forgotten.

By 1860 Jersey City's four wards contained grossly disparate populations. The first and second, the smallest and closest to the ferries, contained about five thousand people each. The large third and fourth wards each contained almost double that number and were growing rapidly. The legislature, therefore, prepared to divide both wards in half, and in each case drew the lines to minimize Irish influence. In the third ward, where the Irish had begun to attain political impact, the line cut north and south, dividing a predominantly Irish community in and around a swamp from a largely native-born community on higher ground. In the 1865 state census the third ward was heavily native-born, and the new sixth ward was heavily immigrant. In dividing the fourth ward, a line drawn directly west from the river to the city's western boundary created one ward only a few blocks wide but over a mile long. The two new wards also contained native-born and Irish areas, but in different proportion, and native-born voters could dominate both. In one case a large Irish community was set off by itself, and in another, Irish voters were divided into two wards and could control neither. While the rationale for neither division received public discussion, the effect could hardly have been accidental.[4]

More than ward boundaries changed in 1861. In the April election Irish voters succeeded in defeating a Know-Nothing recorder and substituting a man closer to themselves. Justice worked unfortunately for the Irish in Jersey City; the enforcement of the liquor laws appeared discriminatory, and Irishmen fell afoul of the laws more regularly than any other group. The City Marshal's report for November 1860 illustrates whom the police, a body 62% native-born in 1860, chose to bring before the court for eventual incarceration by the marshal (see Table XX).[*] The marshal, himself a Know-Nothing in 1856, was an elderly War of 1812 veteran and the Recording Scribe of Fidelity Division, Sons of Temperance.[5] His statistical accuracy did not always go unquestioned. In 1857 Father Kelly claimed that Ellis often listed drunks as Irishmen in his reports without asking them their nationality. "When theories are pushed too far," Kelly wrote to the Know-Nothing Hudson County Courier, "such inaccuracies may,

---

[*]Although the Irish constituted 71.8% of those arrested, they also constituted 75.9% of the unskilled labor force. Similarly, the native-born represented 18.7% of the arrested and 13.1% of the unskilled. Justice worked against the poor, and the poor were Irish, again illustrating the relationship between class and ethnicity.

without much difficulty, be accounted for."[6]

The recorder in 1861 was Thomas E. Tilden, appointed by the aldermen in 1860 upon the resignation of David Bedford,

TABLE XX

CITY MARSHAL'S REPORT, NOVEMBER 1860

Offense			
Drunk	40	Found in a yard	1
Drunk and disorderly	21	Insanity	1
Drunk and exposing person	1	Stealing	4
Drunk and fighting	6	Passing counterfeit money	1
Drunkard	2	Attempting to steal	1
Drunkard and vagrancy	10	Burglary	2
Disorderly	2	Threatening violence	1
Assault and battery	15	TOTAL	128
Violating city ordinance	1		
Gambling	6	Nativity	
Breaking windows	2	Irish	92 71.8%
Assault	4	Native-born	24 18.7
Fighting	1	English	6 4.7
Entering a house	3	German	4 3.2
Malicious mischief	1	Swedish	1 .8
Petty larceny	2	Colored	1 .8
		TOTAL	128 100.0%

elected to a five-year term in 1856. Tilden had been a Know-Nothing county delegate in 1856 and an alderman from 1856 to 1860. He took his work as Recorder seriously, especially liquor law enforcement. While recognizing that many in the city found the license and Sunday closing laws unreasonable, he nevertheless urged strict police enforcement and vowed to do his part in fully enforcing the laws. In his first quarterly report for 1861 he discussed some of his problems. Inviting the Common Council to visit his court, he described typical scenes. "Men, women and children are brought in the station house every night, and are brought before me in the morning drunk and bloated to such an extent that they are disgusting to look at." There was very little he could do for them, he claimed, other than sentence them to jail for sixty days, and even this was impossible with women: "I have no place to confine the drunken women but the jail. I can imprison the women, but cannot imprison the innocent children; nor can I part the mother from the child. From that fact I am compelled to discharge the women, to come back worse than ever." He demanded a new institution, a work house for drunkards, to which he could sentence whole families. There they "could be made to work for their support and drink the wholesome Passaic water."[7]

The Democratic city convention met two weeks later and over vigorous Irish opposition nominated Tilden for a full term as Recorder. Almost a dozen delegates withdrew at this, among them the entire sixth ward delegation. The secessionists met separately and nominated Cornelius C. Martindale, a forty-eight-year-old Englishman. Born in Leistershire, he had been apprenticed as a tallow chandler at fourteen, then worked as a clerk before emigrating in 1837. After working as a carpenter in New York and in California during the gold rush, he settled down as a bookkeeper in Jersey City. Of lower class origins and close to the immigrant community, he had no ties with temperance or nativism. He was also not Irish, an important factor in gaining non-Irish support.[8] When the Democratic convention met again three days later in an effort to restore harmony by rescinding Tilden's nomination in favor of Martindale, the resolution only lost on a tie vote. With no hope of influencing the Democratic nomination, the seceeders then organized the People's Convention to ratify Martindale's nomination and to nominate other candidates for city offices. A week later a committee purporting to represent the German community met and endorsed the Republican candidate for Mayor and Martindale for Recorder. The Republican nominee for Recorder, Henry D. Holt, an abolitionist and, more importantly, a twenty-year member of the Sons of Temperance, was a candidate as unacceptable to the beer-drinking German community as was Tilden.[9]

The election resulted in a rousing victory for Martindale and a resounding defeat for the rest of the People's candidates. It illustrated the ability of the immigrant communities and their allies to defeat candidates who posed a direct threat to their ways of life. Martindale's victory was a victory for Jersey City's immigrant poor; through it they captured an office that dealt mainly with the public problems of the poor. Martindale's election also revealed the success of the division of the old third ward that isolated the Irish in the sixth (see Table XXI). Martindale received his smallest percentage in the third ward and his largest in the new sixth. No

TABLE XXI

ELECTION RETURNS FOR RECORDER, 1861

	Tilden Democrat		Holt Republican		Martindale People	
	N	%	N	%	N	%
Ward Three	302	47.6	100	15.8	232	36.6
Ward Six	55	12.3	13	2.9	378	84.8
Citywide	1008	30.9	462	14.2	1787	54.9

other People's candidate came close to victory. Joseph G. Edge, the mayoralty candidate, received but 18.5% of the vote. The existence of the ticket itself caused comment outside the city, however, with the Newark Mercury reporting Jersey City politics "in a sadly confused state," with one ticket "wholly composed of Irishmen"--a charge that the American Standard vigorously denied.[10]

The difference between Tilden and Martindale was drawn more sharply in 1866 when Tilden ran again, this time as a Republican, facing Martindale, nominated by the Democrats, who could adjust to reality. The Daily Times, successor to the Courier and Advertiser as the Republican paper, demanded "inflexible administration of justice" and noted that Tilden "was always able to find a law to punish criminals . . . which cannot be said of all who have filled that office." Noting that the Recorder's office needed "reforming," the editor continued, "We want a man in that place who understands his business, and is not afraid to do his whole duty. Mr. Tilden . . . will be a terror to evil doers."[11] When the <u>Jersey City Herald</u> reviewed Martindale's career in a sympathetic sketch in 1870, it stressed, in contradistinction to inflexibility, his "considerate and impartial" behavior:

> He is never austere to any poor criminal that is brought before him. He tempers justice with mercy, and his keen knowledge of human nature suits him well to his position. He certainly does not believe in human nature being infallible, and he lectures those brought before him in a kind, fatherly way.[12]

Martindale did not run for a third term in 1871. Before the April election, the state legislature, in a sweeping revision of the city charter, abolished the office and replaced it with two police justices appointed by the legislature itself. These two state appointees carried out their duty in a manner worthy of Recorder Tilden: a year later both were censured by a Hudson County grand jury for the harshness of their punishments.[13]

The harshness Recorder Tilden expressed toward the city's drinking immigrants led to his defeat in 1861. In 1862 the same coalition replaced a Know-Nothing police chief with an Irishman. The 1861 legislature had changed the method of choosing a chief from aldermanic appointment to popular election, with the first election scheduled for April 1862. An Irish push within the Democratic party resulted in the nomination and election of Edward D. Reily, a second-generation Irish Catholic, as chief. Born in Jersey City, Reily was in business for himself as a painter and had been elected an alderman in April 1861 and an assemblyman the following November. At the Democratic convention in March 1862, he sought and received the nomination, defeating Joseph McManus, an Irish Protestant convert, by one vote.[14] In the election that followed, Reily was opposed by Republican Know-Nothing Jacob Z. Marinus, police chief since 1859. The same election saw two native-born Know-Nothing merchants compete for the mayoralty-- Democrat John D. Romar and Republican Hosea F. Clark. Romar and Reily both won. But while Romar got 59.7% of the total vote, Reily received only 51.6%. About 260 people who voted for Romar scratched their tickets when they got to police chief and supported a native-born Protestant over a second-generation Irish Catholic.[15]

Reily died of consumption after serving two years of his three-year term. The aldermen replaced him with one of their own number, Irish-born Patrick Jordon, who had once been on the police force. Jordon's appointment received little comment in the press, yet it provides insights into how the city's politics interacted with its social fabric. As Reily died in late April, the aldermen replaced him at their organizational meeting in early May at which all appointive municipal offices were filled. The Common Council contained thirteen Democrats and five Republicans. Six of the thirteen Democrats were Irish and seven were native-born. But the five most important appointments all went to native-born men. The marshal, city treasurer, collector of revenue, and comptroller had all been Know-Nothings, and Overseer of the Poor William Whitley was no friend of the Irish. But the Irish began to appear on the list of appointees with the offices of street commissioner and city weigher and measurer. Although these appointments were made without comment, it seems likely that the Irish aldermen, in return for the police chief, supported native-born Democrats for the offices dealing with taxation and city institutions.[16]

When Jordon's term expired the following spring, the Democratic convention put him in nomination over Joseph McManus, the Irish Protestant who had lost the nomination three years before. Immediately after Jordon's nomination, however, six delegates, three of whom had been Know-Nothings, walked out in protest. The Republican convention then nominated McManus, and in the election that followed,

Democrats swept every elective office in the city except that of police chief. Here an Irish Protestant defeated an Irish Catholic incumbent for the office. Irishmen were beginning to dominate the police force, and opposition to an Irish force was growing rapidly.[17]

Opposition came to a head in January 1866 with a movement to remove the police force from local control and transfer it to a state-appointed commission. The rhetoric used to justify the change seldom mentioned Irishmen, but the effect of the change was sharply to limit Irish influence in police matters and to increase enforcement of the liquor laws. The commission movement originated among the city's native-born elite, who wished to transfer law enforcement back to men like themselves, men who were at least middle class, Protestant, and temperate. While the percentage of Irishmen on the force seems to have risen markedly between 1860 and 1866, the demand for police "reform" was hardly new and the charge that police positions were patronage doled out by the aldermen dated back to at least 1860. That police behavior was not always of a professional nature was indicated in a letter to the <u>American Standard</u> in the winter of 1860:

> MR. EDITOR:--Will you please to inform me whether members of the police have an immunity whereby they may commit a nuisance in the public streets? One of these uniformed gentry unblushingly committed such a nuisance against the gate of a private

house in York street, last evening, and if he attempts it again is likely to meet a warm reception. Please say if you think that this will make us liable for "interfering with an officer in the performance of his duty."[18]

Late in January 1866, the <u>Jersey City Daily Times</u> demanded that the police department be "elevated above being, as it has long been, a mere political machine run by certain Aldermen for the advancement of their personal interests." Only a commission of responsible men could purify the force of the "foul corruption that now seeks to control it," and these men could only assume power if appointed by a moral agency outside the city, such as the state legislature.[19] Shortly thereafter the legislature began to consider a bill to create the Hudson River Police District, which would transfer police administration to three commissioners appointed by the legislature itself.

Three issues led to the demand for a changed force. First, since 1860, the police force had become increasingly Irish and Catholic. Integrally related was the fear, in the minds of many native-born citizens, that their property was unsafe in the hands of a lower class, immigrant police force, and that the liquor laws and Sabbath ordinances were not enforced by Catholic policemen. Assemblyman Obadiah D. Falkenbury, a Jersey City Republican, urged his fellow legislators to approve the bill, explaining it in terms of the religious persuasion of the police themselves. "Life and property /are/ unsafe in Jersey City," he claimed on the floor of the legislature. "The police /are/ a politico-religious society, and that society in a minority. Pass this bill and it will put down 700 rum holes."[20] The implications here are clear. If the legislature would change those in charge of the force, the commissioners would change the men on the beat. They, in turn, would change at least the public behavior of tipplers and the disorderly. Urging bi-partisan support from "our solid men, our men of intelligence, of business, men who care more for good order than for party," the <u>Daily Times</u> branded those who opposed the commission as "<u>opponents of good government and reform</u>."[21]

The opposition in Jersey City was led by Mayor Orestes Cleveland, a Know-Nothing from 1856 to 1859, and a Democrat thereafter. Born in rural New York in 1829, Cleveland migrated around 1845 to New York, where he worked as a jeweler, and moved to Jersey City soon after. His political career began after he married a daughter of Joseph Dixon, a wealthy manufacturer, and he served as an alderman from 1861 to 1864, and then as mayor from 1864 to 1867. Not completely sympathetic with temperance, his obituary described him as "always a temperate man in the spiritual sense, but, as he remarked frequently, 'He could be one of the boys when he was out with them.'"[22] On the same day that the <u>Daily Times</u> called for a police commission,

Cleveland called for a less radical police reform. Acknowledging that the police must be "entirely removed from the political contests of the day," he proposed a board consisting of the chief, the street inspector, and the president of the Common Council. "The system of taking away the right of self-government from cities, and transferring the governing power to the State Executive, that is now being agitated," he wrote, "is a step backward in the progress of civilization, and should be resisted by every man who approves of a republican form of government."[23]

Cleveland was aware that using state commissions to circumvent local voters when they perversely elected the "wrong" people was not new. New York City's native-born elite had petitioned for and received a state-appointed commission in 1857, passed by a coalition of Know-Nothings and Republicans, and immediately after the Civil War many cities, including Baltimore, Chicago, and Detroit, lost control of their police forces.[24] The purpose was to limit immigrant and Catholic influence in the sensitive matters of law enforcement and the administration of justice. In Jersey City the elected police chiefs and the recorder were all the "wrong" men. Soon after enacting the police commission, Jersey City Republicans urged abolishing the elected Recorder's office, although this was not accomplished for another five years.[25] Jersey City's police commission must be put in the context of post-

Civil War moral reform that sought to extend the concept of centralized national administration to the local level. The <u>Hudson County Democrat</u> connected the police commission with the "unflagging zeal" of Republicans "to concentrate power in the hands of a few men:"

> To Mr. Lincoln it gave authority never conferred upon a monarch; and in the states, whenever and wherever it had the opportunity and ability, it has studiously deprived democratic municipalities of their chartered rights and vested them in one man, . . . to reduce our township and city governments to a perfect serfdom.$_{26}$

Leonidas Abbett, a Hudson County assemblyman, led the opposition in the state legislature.* Like Cleveland, he couched his opposition in terms of local control of local institutions; that centralized administration held more dangers than an immigrant government. "Don't trample on the rights of the people," Abbett urged the legislature, don't allow "this gradual attempt to centralize power." Abbett had opposed the increased powers assumed by the

---

*Born in Philadelphia, the son of a journeyman hatter, Abbett became a lawyer, moved to Hoboken, and began a law practice in New York City. He was first elected to the assembly in 1865, and again in 1866. Moving to Jersey City in 1867, he played an increasingly important role in local and state politics as assemblyman and senator in the 1870's, and in 1883 as governor. During the 1870's Abbett was one of the few people who succeeded in holding the confidence and trust of both the native-born and Irish Democrats. Richard A. Hogarty, "Leon Abbett of New Jersey: Precursor of the Modern Governor" (Ph. D. Dissertation, Princeton, 1966), pp. 30-32.

federal government to fight the Civil War and which culminated in Radical reconstruction. The Republicans were "the corrupt and revolutionary party" embarking on a course of "Congressional usurpation." When Andrew Johnson vetoed the Freedman's Bureau Bill, Abbett introduced a resolution into the Assembly to fire a 100-gun salute. As a state legislator, he opposed the reconstruction of the Jersey City police force for much the same reasons that he opposed Reconstruction of the South: it violated fundamental concepts of local control of local institutions, and concentrated power beyond the reach of popular checks.[27] Neither Abbett nor Cleveland defended Irishmen, Catholics, or "rum holes." Although the police commission was clearly directed at all three, native-born opposition revolved around concepts of traditional municipal prerogatives and the appropriateness of an outside body regulating the police in Jersey City.

Two weeks after the commission bill was presented in the legislature, Mayor Cleveland called a public meeting scheduled for February 17, 1866. Chaired by Cleveland, the meeting was tumultuous. Zebina K. Pangborn, editor of the *Daily Times*, and Jacob Weart, the reputed author of the bill, spoke in favor of the commission, emphasizing the need for a non-political force. But Pangborn also went out of his way to assure his audience that the new force would apply the law equally to rich and poor. The opponents conceded the need for reform, but stressed the loss of local control over the spending of taxes. Very few speakers--on either side--completed their remarks without interruption. The meeting ended with lengthy resolutions repudiating the commission as an "unnecessary attempt to take from us our chartered rights." The police, the resolution held, might exercise "absolute power over citizens which in excited political times might be used for party purposes and to the detriment of good order and the oppression of citizens." Here was fear of a police itself.[28] Noting that those Irishmen who attended the meeting had opposed the commission, the Daily Times interpreted this as further evidence of the need for a new police force:

> The great bulk of the adherents of the Mayor were of that class that always votes the "dimycrat" ticket, less than a half dozen of the well-known and heavy taxpaying citizens being among them. When the house divided, the contrast of the two crowds was most suggestive. If any further evidence had been wanting of the necessity and wisdom of the proposed change contemplated by the Police bill, a single look at the audience thus divided would have furnished it.

It was "an immense majority of the more intelligent, wealthy and taxpaying citizens of Jersey City" who were "earnestly in favor" of a police commission.[29]

The resolutions passed at the public meeting instructed

the Mayor to appoint a committee to study the police problem, and, if necessary, to go to Trenton to lobby against the bill. Cleveland did appoint a committee, but it was never heard from again. The nature of the men he appointed, however, suggests rather strongly that his own conception of moral order was hardly different from those supporting the commission. All five men were native-born, and at least nominal Democrats. The group included the president of the Hudson County Bible Society, the president of the City Mission and Tract Society, and two men who had, at various times, served on the Board of Managers of both organizations. The fifth was a lawyer specializing in bank problems.[30] This committee, then, consisted largely of men who were themselves active in preserving and extending a Protestant conception of order. While opposing a state-appointed police commission as a means to this end, they certainly agreed with Assemblyman Falkenbury that life and property were unsafe in Jersey City. The Irish, against whom the commission was directed, had no place in the organized opposition. The native-born opponents of the commission were themselves too much a part of the same culture to compromise publicly with rum and Romanism.

The bill passed through the Republican-controlled state legislature with little difficulty. In the Assembly,

Leon Abbett offered two amendments, which were defeated in succession: the first would have made the office of police commissioner elective; the second would have postponed the institution of an appointive board until the system was ratified by the Jersey City electorate. In the Senate, Charles Winfield, the Hudson County representative, agreed that the power to appoint policemen be removed from the Common Council, but suggested instead a police commission appointed by the Mayor. A state-appointed commission would be "tyranny and despotism." A Republican spokesman responded, however, that "many of the first and best people" of Jersey City, from both parties, had demanded "that the power of appointing policemen should be taken away from the local authorities depending upon popular favor."[31]

The Senate approved the bill in late March by a party-line vote, and it was signed into law by Governor Marcus L. Ward, who then nominated the three commissioners for quick ratification by the legislature. John W. Pangborn, the brother of the Daily Times's editor, came from Vermont and had been in the city less than five years. A notions merchant in New York, he had been the Republican candidate for mayor in 1863 and was a staunch temperance man. Isaac W. Scudder, a lawyer, came from an old New Jersey family and had served as Hudson County District

Attorney. The third man, Henry Finck, ran a restaurant and saloon in New York City and had an interest in a large Hoboken beer hall. As one of the commission's most important purposes was temperance, he would be criticized for attempting to serve "those two opposing interests, the Temperance Societies and the Liquor Dealers Association."[32] All three men were Protestant and of at least moderate wealth, and Pangborn, elected chairman, was associated with the City Mission and Tract Society.*

The law under which the commissioners operated created the Hudson River Police District, comprising Jersey City and any other area the legislature decided to include in the future. The manner in which the police force was administered changed drastically, but the powers and functions of the police were not significantly altered. The Commissioners served three-year staggered terms, had to be registered voters of Jersey City, and could hold no other local office. When the term of the elected chief expired, they would appoint a replacement, who, like the patrolmen, would then serve at the commissioners' pleasure. The act set salaries of fifteen hundred dollars for the chief, a three hundred dollar raise; dropped the four

---

*Seven years later, when John Pangborn was a member of the school board and embroiled in a dispute with the city's Catholics, the Irish World referred to him as "one of those who have never left the Know-Nothing harness." May 10, 1873.

aides from one thousand to eight hundred and fifty dollars; and left patrolmen at eight hundred, their salary under the old force. To raise the necessary funds, the commissioners met annually with the chairman of the Common Council's Finance Committee and the police chief as a Board of Estimate. But if the Common Council refused requests, the commissioners had the power to assess taxes directly. They were indeed independent of the elected municipal administration.[33]

Before they made Jersey City a more temperate and orderly city, the commissioners had to establish their legitimacy. Although sworn in as state officials in early April, Mayor Cleveland and the Common Council refused to acknowledge the legality of the act creating the new force. Edward F. C. Young, the city treasurer, refused to honor checks written by Pangborn but honored those signed by the Mayor, who continued as head of the old force. Thus for over two months Jersey City had two police forces: that of the Mayor and that of the commissioners. The result was a virtual collapse of police responsibility as each attempted to countermand the other. Not until June 25th did the commissioners obtain a mandamus compelling Young to honor their drafts, and an injunction restraining Cleveland from continuing the old force.[34]

The commissioners' first business was to organize a

force of fifty men, the legal maximum, and about 25% larger than its predecessor. While the composition of the force in early 1866 is unknown, the *Daily Times* printed the name, age and place of birth of the forty-eight men hired by late July 1866. The papers made it clear that many Irish men were not rehired; indeed a major purpose of the commission was to re-Protestantize the force. The commission succeeded in reducing the percentage of Irish to that of 1860. Table XXII compares the new force of July 1866 with the force as it appeared in the 1860 census.[35] While the new force contained but a bare majority of native-born men, Irish removals still caused comments

TABLE XXII

JERSEY CITY POLICEMEN BY NATIVITY, 1860 AND 1866

	1860		1866	
Irish	11	37.9%	19	39.6%
Native-born	18	61.1	26	54.2
German	0	0.0	3	6.2
British	0	0.0	0	0.0
TOTAL	29	100.0%	48	100.0%

in nearby towns. The *Hudson City Union* quipped, "Have you been to Jersey City lately? Jersey City has a police--a new police--no Irish admitted!"[36]

The new force was also younger than that of 1860. By refusing to appoint men over fifty, the commission dropped the average age from thirty-six to thirty-three years. Although most appointees were believed to be Republican in politics, the new force was not a repository for superannuated campaign workers. How well the new force could enforce the temperance laws caused some question. Still basically a night watch, thirty-eight patrolmen were detailed to the night shift and only six to the day shift. They had no power of summary arrest and no extra men for Sunday duty. Keeping qualified men must also have been a problem. The following year the legislature raised the patrolmen's salaries from eight hundred to one thousand dollars and specified that appointees must have been residents of the United States for five years.[37]

In early July, two weeks after the police commissioners assumed their duties, the Common Council received a petition with a reported 3970 signatures calling for better enforcement of the Sabbath laws. This petition had its roots in legislation passed by the New York legislature for New York City. On May 1, 1866, a stiff excise law went into effect which had the effect of closing down New York City on Sundays. Not surprisingly, thousands of New Yorkers ferried to the saloons of Jersey City and the beer gardens of Hoboken and Hudson City. Although "a generally orderly class of people," they excited a push in Jersey City for Sunday closing enforcement.[38] During May and June, the police were immobilized by the competing claims of Mayor Cleveland and the police commissioners. Not until July could an organized movement against Sunday drinking possibly go into effect, and even then nothing happened. The Common Council sat on the petition for two months and then quietly referred the problem to the Police Commission. The commissioners claimed a lack of authority; the problems of making arrests only after applying to the City Recorder for a warrant frustrated their endeavors, and they recommended that the Council revise its ordinances to allow summary arrest in liquor cases. The Council replied that the commissioners had power enough, and would pass no new ordinances. Here matters sat for six months until the spring of 1867.[39]

In the April 1867 mayoralty election Jersey City voters again demonstrated the power of nativism over party allegiance when a Republican former Know-Nothing, James Gopsill, defeated Charles H. O'Neill, the first Irishman to run for mayor in Jersey City. When the Democratic convention met during the first week in April, it found the nomination for Mayor an unsought prize, and difficult to give away. Incumbent Orestes Cleveland, to whom it was offered by acclamation, turned it down, citing business pressures. Wealthy real estate owner John Van Vorst likewise declined. A divided convention then turned to Charles H. O'Neill. Two days later the Republican convention enacted a similar charade, nominating Daniel McLeod and James L. Ogden, both New York businessmen, before finding a reluctant candidate in James Gopsill, the secretary of a local insurance company.[40]

Charles O'Neill and James Gopsill had much in common. Both were native-born, the sons of immigrants, and both had moved to Jersey City when adults. Both were successful businessmen, and both advocated and practiced temperance. Here the similarity ended. O'Neill, a lumber merchant, was of Irish parentage and a staunch Catholic. Gopsill, the son of English Quakers, was a founding member of the First Presbyterian Church and had entered politics through the Know-Nothing movement in the 1850's. Both were politically experienced. O'Neill had served as a county Freeholder for two years and as an alderman for two years. As a chairman of the Finance Committee of the Common Council, he had won acclaim as a sound, conservative manager of the city finances. Gopsill had never held political office, but had worked in numerous Republican campaigns, and was active in the successful attempt in 1867 to delete the word "white" from the New Jersey constitution.[41]

Nominations were concluded on April 7; the election took place on April 9. Although there was no campaign as such, the election results, and events shortly thereafter,

indicate the strength of religious and ethnic tension in
Jersey City immediately after the Civil War. O'Neill lost
because he was Irish and Catholic and could not prevent
the defection of native-born Democrats to his opponent.
Gopsill carried the four wards that showed a majority of
native-born males sixteen or over in the state census of
1865, and lost the three with a foreign-born majority.[42]
The Democratic American Standard, whose nativist editor
gave O'Neill no support at all, blamed his defeat on
Democrats who put "personal prejudices" before "the principles of the party" and either stayed home or voted
Republican. The Daily Times credited Gopsill's victory
"to the fact that our best citizens, who have the largest
stake in this community, gave him their support, irrespective of party preference." In a letter to the New York
Sun a year later, James W. O'Brien, an Irish Catholic,
concurred. O'Neill lost because of "the defection of
ex-Know-Nothings, high in the party."[43]

The best evidence of the Know-Nothing roots behind
Gopsill's political flowering came from the Mayor-elect
himself. A week after his election Gopsill was serenaded
by a brass band and a crowd of "citizens of both sexes"
at his home. He spoke to the crowd and expressed both
his thanks and his personal political beliefs. He began
with a declaration of his party loyalty: "I am a member

of the Republican party, in full communion and a sincere believer in the principles and policy it advocated and sustained during the five years of long and bloody war . . . ." Praising the party of Lincoln at length, he then abruptly changed course:

> While I admit . . . that I owe my election primarily to the Republican party, I would be ungrateful did I not acknowledge my obligations to the hundreds of American Democrats, among whom I have grown up, with whom I have associated in by-gone times, who know me through and through, and who from personal preference or personal love and regard, gave me their votes—to them I owe a debt of gratitude I can never repay because they were bound by no party ties to give me their support.[44]

Gopsill thus acknowledged the Know-Nothing heritage of himself and his friends of "by-gone times." He then turned to the Protestantism which he and his serenaders also shared, and articulated a conviction and offered a pledge which would dominate his administration of Jersey City:

> To the Christian community of all denominations and to the members of our various Temperance Associations who manifested so much interest in my success, need I say to them that I will exercise all the official power I may possess to protect, preserve and defend the sanctity of the Christian Sabbath and circumscribe the fearful vice of rum selling.[45]

To Gopsill, a primary function of local government was to preserve and protect Christian institutions as defined by evangelical Protestantism, and to subordinate non-evangelicals to a definition of order other than their own. A quiet Sabbath symbolized this subordination of non-evangelicals--of Irish Catholics and German "infidels"--to Protestant morality. The religious overtones were obvious. The class overtones--that most Irish Catholics were poor and most native-born Protestants were not--were equally obvious, but usually stated, if stated at all, within a religious framework. Gopsill considered the saloons of Jersey City "pestiferous holes" that "create and foster nearly all the evils which populate our prisons and almshouses," places which "but for the beastly habit of dram drinking . . . would be rendered almost superfluous."[46] Poverty was neither an economic nor a social problem. It was a moral problem.

When Gopsill assumed office on May 1, 1867, he had at his disposal a strengthened police commission. The legislature of 1867 had bestowed upon the Hudson River Police District the power of summary arrest in cases involving violations of the Sunday and liquor laws. The commissioners had received the power the lack of which, they had claimed the previous fall, made it impossible for the police to function effectively. Gopsill called the new powers "a source of great rejoicing" which would "ensure us a quiet and orderly Sabbath."[47] The chairmanship of the Police Commission had also changed hands.

John Pangborn resigned, because of business pressures, and the governor replaced him with Obadiah D. Falkenbury, the legislator who had denounced the city police as a "politico-religious organization" and stressed the need for suppressing "rum holes." Falkenbury, like Gopsill, had entered the Republican party through the Know-Nothing movement. "Sunday rum selling," intoned the Daily Times, "so far as he can reach it, will receive its quietus from him."[48]

Good weather in the spring of 1867 again brought thirsty New Yorkers to the Jersey banks of the Hudson. A New York Sun reporter in Hoboken thought that "generally speaking" they were "of the orderly class of people who go out on Sunday for a day of rational enjoyment after the labor and confinement of the week." Another reporter saw them as "the laboring classes, with their wives and children," who "go in and get a glass or two of lager, and a bit of bread and cheese." In Hoboken, "the greatest liberty prevails." In equally libertarian Hudson City a petition to enforce the Sunday laws was referred by the Common Council to the police, but with the qualification that "they think . . . the enforcement of the State laws undesirable, as it would stop all worldly business, and probably victimize the petitioners as well as others."[49]

In Jersey City the greatest liberty was not to prevail. On Saturday, May 4th, three days after Gopsill's inauguration, the police commission ordered each patrolman on duty on Sunday to "note every case where any person or persons shall expose for sale, or sell, within the limits of Jersey City, any spiritous, vinous, fermented, or other intoxicating liquors . . . ." The Liquor Dealers Association acquiesced, and there was but one reported violation. The papers reported no crowds of thirsty New Yorkers in Jersey City. Round number one went to Gopsill.[50]

Round two opened one week later. The police were ordered to arrest anyone doing business on Sunday, excepting hotel keepers serving food to their own boarders, and druggists dispensing drugs. Although this conformed to a city ordinance of 1862, it contravened a state law of 1846 which allowed restaurants to remain open "for the use of sojourners, travelers, and strangers." As a transportation center, Jersey City had more than its share of all three. One of them caught the ear of a reporter:

> "Do you call this Republicanism, justice, or even humanity? I say it's infamous. And then the newspapers they will say tomorrow there was another 'quiet Sunday in Jersey City.' Quiet--yes, but they don't take any account of the dissatisfied rumbling beneath every man's waistcoat pocket. It's a scandal!"[51]

On the following day eleven cases came before Recorder Cornelius Martindale involving infractions of the Sabbatarian regulations. But Martindale, elected by the Irish and German communities in 1861 and in 1866, refused to cooperate, and through one means or another, succeeded in dismissing all eleven cases. Most arrests involved the mere exposure of liquor without proof of sale or intent to sell. These were dismissed immediately, and Martindale served notices that similar cases would receive similar treatment: "'I took a ground here when I first came on this liquor business, and I have not deviated from it yet, nor do I intend to do so. I have never supposed that the mere exposure of liquor is a sufficient ground for me to entertain a complaint.'" The evidence in one case was empty glasses with wet bottoms on top of a bar, the original contents unknown. Case dismissed. Another arrest involved a druggist accused of selling licorice to a small girl. Martindale ruled that licorice--on Sunday in Jersey City at least--was a drug and therefore exempt. Case dismissed.[52]

This disdain for temperance raised to the level of coercion largely accounted for Martindale's popularity among Jersey City's immigrant population who had placed him in office. He explicitly removed himself from the new police policy: "The Police Commissioners are now an independent body in the government of the city, and they are determined to make these arrests, and I have no power to direct an officer to do anything." He found unwise not only the policy but also the police power that made it possible. Summary arrest, Martindale claimed, violated the due-process-of-law provisions of both the United States and New Jersey constitutions, and in these cases he placed personal liberty before public order. The police commissioners countered by avoiding Martindale's court and, on subsequent Sundays, took offenders to local Justices of the Peace.[53]

The severity of Gopsill's Sunday closing crusade drew criticism from the friends of temperance as well as its opponents. Zebina K. Pangborn, now editing the Evening Journal, felt that such rigid enforcement would bring even reasonable measures into disrepute, and Judge Bedle told the spring grand jury that commissioners could be indicted if, in their zeal, they had violated any laws. Gradually enforcement eased and before too long one could buy a meal, if not a drink, on Sunday in Jersey City.[54]

Gopsill began his crusade to limit saloons and liquor stores by vetoing all licenses passed by the Common Council that did not meet his own stringent, extra-legal standard. He attempted to deny licenses to any storekeeper who proposed to sell commodities other than liquor, and all women. Charles O'Neill led the opposition in the Common Council and found Gopsill's standards unrealistic and discriminatory. Finding no point in restricting liquor to stores selling nothing else, he had but one test: "If the applicant were respectable, he would vote for him." Using this test, O'Neill led the Common Council in overriding most vetoes.[55] Gopsill took these defeats not as one reasonable view prevailing over one differing, but as political cowardice on the part of the aldermen who had sold their souls for office. He taunted them in an address in January 1868:

> . . . And yet is it not pitiful to see a citizen otherwise estimable, bow down to the moloch of rum in order to obtain political power--is it not humiliating to see a professing Christian sell his religion and his Savior for the vote emanating from the grog-shop and the cockpit.[56]

The aldermen, he claimed, had licensed "hundreds of groggeries" which were "the resort of prostitutes, thieves and pick-pockets." And the Sabbath was "trodden underfoot by nearly all engaged in this hellish traffic in rum."[57]

The City Mission and Tract Society, long associated with temperance and nativism, sought to mobilize public support for Gopsill, and in mid-July 1867 staged a monster rally endorsing the policies of the Mayor and the police commissioners. Trumpeted in the press for days in advance, the meeting was presided over by Bennington F. Randolph, president of the Hudson County Bible Society and also the president of the Jersey City Board of Education. For assistance he had 164 vice presidents and 32 secretaries, including the Protestant elite of both political parties. Of the 164 vice presidents, at least thirty--almost twenty percent--had been in the Know-Nothing movement of the 1850's, and many others were identified with other nativist organizations. The speeches emphasized the relationship between the municipal government and the preservation of morality. The Rev. Lewis R. Dunn traced in mythic form the legal history of the Christian Sabbath. It "was a part of the common law of the land; it was a part of the common law of England before our Pilgrim fathers crossed the sea . . . ." And on it American liberties rested: "If the Christian Sabbath were removed from us for ten years and if there were substituted for it the European Sabbath, our free institutions would be undermined and destroyed." Bennington F. Randolph praised the firmness of the Mayor, the police, and the grand jury, and stressed the need for them to continue the institutionalization of virtue: "This is no organization," he told the assembled multitude, "--we need none. The law is our basis for organization."[58]

No figure associated with Catholic temperance appeared on the program, and the headline in the *Daily Times*, "Law and Order Triumphant," indicated that temperance symbolized more than the mere absence of liquor. Six of the eight speakers had a history of outspoken condemnation of things Irish and Catholic, and the rally is best understood as an attempt by native-born Protestants to assert publicly that their conception of order would prevail in the community through the coercion that control of the municipal machinery allowed.[59]

They were at least partially successful. Although the Common Council continued to license saloons through the summer and fall, the police commissioners felt that they, at least, were doing their job, and they said so in their annual report to the legislature.

> Sundays have been as they should be--quiet, peaceable, and respected. The liquor saloons have been closed, not as the proprietors desired, from 10 until 1 o'clock, but as the Commissioners ordered, from 12 o'clock Saturday night until 12 o'clock Sunday night.[60]

Gopsill's term as Mayor came to an end in April 1868, and he stood for re-election. His opponent, again, was Charles H. O'Neill. The election was similar to that of 1867, with the exception that the Democratic party united more solidly behind O'Neill, and this carried him to victory. The reasons for this are obscure. When the New York Sun endorsed Gopsill because of his temperance record, James W. O'Brien wrote in reply that O'Neill was "pre-eminently a friend of sobriety," and that "law and order have no firmer friend." He blamed O'Neill's 1867 defeat on "the defection of ex-Know-Nothings," but stated forcibly that "at this time the treachery is not likely to be repeated." Perhaps the discomfiture of liquor dealers of all ethnic stripes, or the threat of an Irish bolt on other issues, forced native-born Democrats to swallow Charles O'Neill.[61]

O'Neill campaigned as a voice of moderation. "We have had enough of radicalism, fanaticism and hypocrisy," he announced in his acceptance of the nomination, "enough of fanatical legislation." The *American Standard* gave its support this time, and set the candidate in the general framework of post-Civil War politics by waving the bloodied Constitution: Charles O'Neill is opposed to the so-called 'Higher Law' that teaches disobedience to the Constitution and the laws as interpreted by the proper tribunals."[62] Thus was O'Neill separated intellectually from Theodore Parker, Charles Sumner, and James Gopsill.

Gopsill's friends defended his record vigorously. At a rally on the night before the election, Zebina K. Pangborn played subtly on the religious and ethnic issue by claiming that if O'Neill were elected, "Jersey City next summer will be a second edition of Hoboken." Gopsill spoke on his own behalf. "Is law, is order, is the Sabbath of any consequence to you?" he asked his audience. "If so, I ask you in God's name to preserve it. I think . . . that victory is sure," he concluded, "and with that assurance I commit our cause to God and the people."[63]

If God voted in Jersey City, however, he cast only one ballot. O'Neill squeezed out a narrow victory and a year of temperance administration came to an end. Jersey City's non-evangelical population demonstrated once again that it could defeat a candidate directly antagonistic to its interests. Although an abstainer himself, O'Neill would not seek to force others to follow his example. "I am convinced," he wrote in his annual message to the Common Council, "that so long as rum is manufactured it will be drank /sic/ and when people want rum they are bound to have it, and if not through the front door, they will find a side door very soon."[64] Favoring a high license fee to offset the evils of liquor ("I am convinced that the indiscriminate use of intoxicating drinks . . . is the principal source whence come our paupers."), O'Neill felt that any reputable person should be able to procure a license.[65]

O'Neill also had a new police commission with which to deal. The 1868 legislature, controlled by Democrats, threw out the Republican Hudson River Police Commission and replaced it with a Democratic Jersey City Police Commission. The change, however, did not change the type of men appointed. All three were native-born and two had been Know-Nothings.[66] The bill provided, however, that each year one commission seat would become elective. In

1869 Matthew Monks, an Irish Catholic hatter, defeated John Edelstein, a native-born shop-keeper.[67]

The new commission, under Democratic pressure to appoint Democrats, and one-third Irish after 1869, appointed more Irish to the force. Table XXIII compares the nativity of the police in 1866 under the Hudson River Police Commission with the force as it existed on May 1, 1870,

TABLE XXIII

JERSEY CITY POLICEMEN BY NATIVITY, 1866 AND 1870

	1866		1870	
Irish	19	39.6%	40	65.6%
Native-born	26	54.2	18	29.6
German	3	6.2	1	1.6
British	0	0.0	2	3.2
TOTAL	48	100.0%	61	100.0%

just before another major change in city administration.[68] As the commissioners became elective, the electorate chose Irish commissioners, and they, in turn, appointed more Irish to the force.

Through the 1860's Jersey City's Irish began to enter the political life of the city. Attempting to influence those city institutions in which they came into closest contact, they sought first to influence the administration of justice. First electing a recorder, then a police chief, and finally a mayor, the immigrant communities sought to mitigate the influence of evangelical Protestantism and anti-Catholicism in city government. In 1866 the Protestant community responded by appealing to the state legislature for state-appointed officials to run the police force. After 1868 the commission gradually became elective and the force again became predominantly Irish. The native-born Protestants were fighting the force of numbers as immigrants became naturalized and entered the electorate. While many immigrants, chiefly the British, the Protestant Irish and the evangelical Germans, did support the native-born elite in both parties, they were outnumbered by the Catholic Irish and non-evangelical Germans. To the native-born elite, it was this "immigrant vote" that defeated their candidates. Between 1868 and 1870 the native-born elite lost control of Jersey City.

DOCUMENTATION: CHAPTER IV

[1] *Standard*, August 11, 1859.

[2] *Courier and Advertiser*, September 5, 1860.

[3] *Standard*, March 14, 1860.

[4] *Ibid.*, March 1, 1861. For census, see *Ibid.*, September 12, 1865.

[5] *Ibid.*, December 1, 1860; *Jersey City Times*, May 20, 1867.

[6] *Hudson County Courier*, July 23, 1857. Kelly had responded to Dunning's comments on the marshal's report. Dunning felt that there would be fewer drunken Irishmen if the priests, "who are known to exercise almost absolute control over them," would only do their duty. *Ibid.*, July 9, 1857.

[7] *Standard*, March 14, 1861. Despite these views, Tilden said of himself in court, "I am not a fanatic on any subject. I am certainly not a temperance fanatic." *Ibid.*, December 18, 1860.

[8] *Ibid.*, March 26, 1861; *Jersey City Herald*, July 9, 1870.

[9] *Standard*, April 2, 1861; *New York World*, April 9, 1861.

[10] *Standard*, April 4, 17, 1861.

[11] *Jersey City Times*, April 6, 7, 1866.

[12] *Jersey City Herald*, July 9, 1870.

[13] *New York Times*, March 12, 1872.

[14] *Standard*, March 27, 1862. McManus had left the Catholic Church over the issue of masonry and was buried a Methodist. *Evening Journal*, December 31, 1868.

[15] *Standard*, April 1, 1862.

[16] *Jersey City Chronicle*, March 19, April 30, 1864; *New York World*, May 3, 1864.

[17] *Standard*, March 30, April 12, 1865.

[18] Courier and Advertiser, July 19, 1860.

[19] Jersey City Times, January 31, 1866.

[20] Standard, February 15, 1866. The paper explained that Falkenbury meant Irish Catholics, and added gratuitously, "A man may be a Catholic and still be a respectable member of society."

[21] Jersey City Times, February 14, 1866; Standard, February 16, 1866.

[22] Jersey City News and Evening Journal, March 31, 1896.

[23] Jersey City Times, January 31, 1866.

[24] James F. Richardson, The New York Police: Colonial Times to 1901 (New York, 1970), pp. 81-89; 123.

[25] Standard, November 19, 1866.

[26] Hudson County Democrat (Hoboken), February 24, 1866.

[27] Standard, February 15, 1866; August 10, 1868; Newark Daily Advertiser, February 7, 23, 1866.

[28] Standard, Jersey City Times, and New York Tribune, February 19, 1866.

[29] Jersey City Times, February 19, 1866.

[30] Standard, February 20, 1866.

[31] Newark Daily Advertiser, February 7, March 2, 1866.

[32] Standard, March 26, October 4, November 19, 1866. The New York Sunday Mercury claimed that Finck also kept a bawdy house at 88 Vesey Street, New York. Ibid., April 30, 1866.

[33] Ibid., March 6, 1866.

[34] Jersey City Times, April 24, June 26, 27, 29, 1866.

[35] Ibid., July 26, 1866.

[36] Quoted in Standard, November 19, 1866.

[37] Costello, pp. 68-70.

[38] *Jersey City Times*, July 5, 1866; *New York World*, May 7, 14, 16, 21, 1866.

[39] *Standard*, October 3, 1866.

[40] *New York Sun*, April 5, 7, 1867.

[41] Biographical information on O'Neill, *Standard*, April 9, 1867, and *Evening Journal*, October 17, 1868. On Gopsill, Shaw, pp. 1145-1146.

[42] *Standard*, September 12, 1865.

[43] *Standard* and *Jersey City Times*, April 10, 1867; *New York Sun*, April 8, 1868.

[44] *Standard*, April 19, 1867.

[45] Ibid.

[46] Annual Message of Mayor Gopsill, *Jersey City Times*, May 15, 1867.

[47] Ibid.

[48] *Jersey City Times*, April 11, 1867.

[49] *New York Sun*, September 30, 1867, October 13, 1867; *New York Freeman's Journal and Catholic Register*, May 25, 1867.

[50] *Jersey City Times*, May 4, 6, 1867; *New York Tribune*, May 4, 1867. The *Times* (May 20, 1867) thought Henry Finck a "most determined and zealous advocate" of temperance enforcement in Jersey City because of his interest in a large beer hall in Hoboken only a few hundred feet from the Jersey City boundary.

[51] *Jersey City Times*, May 13, 1867.

[52] Ibid., May 14, 1867.

[53] Ibid., May 18, 1867.

[54] Ibid., May 27, 1867; *Journal*, May 13, 1867; *Standard*, May 21, 1867.

[55] *Jersey City Times*, May 22, 1867, June-August, *passim*.

[56] *Journal*, January 15, 1868.

[57] Ibid.

[58] Ibid., July 16, 1867.

[59] Jersey City Times, July 16, 1867. The speakers included the Revs. Dunn, Parmley, Cordo, and Harkness; B. F. Randolph, Z. K. Pangborn, and S. B. Ransom (later a Prohibitionist candidate for governor). Many prohibitionists at the meeting were uneasy at endorsing a licensing law. Among the 164 vice presidents were all living former mayors since 1852.

[60] Journal, December 19, 1867.

[61] New York Sun, April 8, 1868.

[62] Standard, April 7, 10, 1868.

[63] Journal, April 14, 1868.

[64] Standard, July 9, 1868.

[65] Ibid.

[66] Journal, February 17, 1868. The new commission also included the mayor and the recorder.

[67] Ibid., April 14, 1869. The Board appointed Nathan B. Fowler, a retired hotel-keeper, as chief. Fowler, born in Albany, New York, was described as having a "Wellington" nose. Jersey City Herald, June 18, 1870.

[68] Jersey City Times, July 26, 1866; May 9, 1870. The new commissioners were installed on March 9, 1868, and were besieged by applicants described as "the sorriest congregation of loafers" who should "attend to their business of 'hod carrying'"--a clear reference to the Irish. Ibid., March 9, 1868.

CHAPTER V

THE TRANSITION TO AN IMMIGRANT CITY
1868 - 1870

Jersey City remained a Democratic city throughout the decade after 1860. Although James Gopsill served as the only Republican mayor, the Common Council was always heavily Democratic. While the proportion of native-born Democrats slowly diminished as more Irishmen gained elective office, nevertheless before 1868 native-born Democrats controlled the party machinery and through it the city. Termed a "ring" by their opponents, a relatively small number of native-born Democrats, many of them Know-Nothings in the 1850's, successfully used Irish votes to keep themselves in or near office. Their problem was to maintain party discipline among native-born and Irish Democrats while retaining control of the decision-making process.

The "ring" can best be approached through its opposition. Republican newspapers continually worked to force a wedge between native-born and Irish Democrats in order to secure support from the latter. Attacks had a standard form. Coupled with reminders of the Know-Nothing past of the leadership went charges of fiscal irresponsibility. Published in 1863, the "Junius" letters were typical.[1] At the center of the "ring," claimed "Junius," was the <u>American Standard</u>, edited by John Lyons, "the high priest of Know-Nothingism" who "still detests anything savoring of 'Irish' and turns up his huge proboscis at the mention of 'Dutch.'" The Irish had been "bamboozled by the great apostle of dark lanterns, and midnight intrigues against our adopted citizens." When Bernard McAnally sought the sheriff's office in 1862, "Junius" claimed, Lyons worked first to defeat the nomination, then to secure the Republican nomination for his own candidate, and finally to defeat McAnally. Although "competent and honest," McAnally was still "Irish and a Mick." "Junius" urged the Irish to remember Lyons's oath "to ostracize every mother's son of an Irishman who dared to aspire to any position higher than hod carrier."[2]

With these attacks went the usual charge that Lyons, as city printer, did far more public printing than was warranted and at inflated rates. The same men who "concocted their plans in the private room at the Standard office" also "managed to secure all the fat offices" and "plundered the city treasury most unmercifully."[3] Although these charges continued through the decade, no hard evidence of corruption surfaced, and no indictments were ever brought against public officials during this period. If there was corruption, it was probably small-time stuff.

The Standard continued to speak only for native-born Democrats, and Lyons played a large but private role in city politics. As editor he walked a thin line, neither appeasing nor outraging the Irish community and never discussing divisions within the party. When the 1866 congressional convention could not agree on a congressional nominee, for example, and degenerated into a brawl between largely native-born and Irish factions, the *Standard* account had the convention peacefully adjourn just before the problems began.[4] For the same reasons, the *Standard* almost never gave biographical information on candidates for office, and it was impossible to tell nationality or religion from the *Standard*'s columns. News about the Irish community received truncated coverage, and news of Catholicism received even less. Only local Fenian activity received coverage in any quantity, and even this was possibly tied to anti-Catholicism. Zebina K. Pangborn, editor of the *Daily Times*, and as anti-Catholic as Lyons, spoke at one and only one Fenian meeting--a meeting to denounce Father Aloysius Vanuta for branding the Fenians "a worthless, reckless and demoralized set of men." The resolutions condemned his "unwarrantable and despotic exercise of assumed authority" over his parishioners, a view thoroughly compatible with Protestant conceptions of Catholicism.[5]

    The local Democratic party offered Irish voters tangible returns not offered by the Republicans. Sunday closing and license laws were not enforced with any regularity under Democratic mayors. Party leaders provided a certain amount of patronage in minor city positions. Between 1860 and 1866 and then again between 1868 and 1870 the police became increasingly Irish, and relatively unimportant ward offices, such as constable, went to the Irish. Party orators used the themes of national politics to boom local candidates, dwelling in particular on the relationship between northern Republicans and southern Negroes. When Leon Abbett endorsed Orestes Cleveland for Congress in 1866, for example, he reminded his listeners that Cleveland "would never vote a dollar for the Freedman's Bureau or to keep an army in the South."[6]

Money also worked to hold the Irish and the native-born together, although this side of party affairs remains yet obscure. Middle class Irishmen claimed in 1870 that the native-born leaders relied upon "the lowest class of Irishmen" to keep themselves in power, and that they "debauch young men and give them money and make them the tools of politicians."[7] After 1868 they claimed that the Democratic police commission used the force to control ward primaries, and in 1870 an Irish splinter group complained that "old residents are hurled from primaries like dogs by uniformed partisans."[8] "Great care has been taken to exclude Irishmen of character and intelligence" from the Board of Aldermen, claimed the Republican <u>Jersey City Times</u>, and when elected, Irish aldermen were kept off important committees and isolated as far as parliamentary procedure would allow.[9] Alderman Michael Connolly was a case in point. Elected from the newly created seventh ward in 1867, Connally pursued an independent course and in consequence the <u>Standard</u> reported his remarks in brogue. Commented the <u>Evening Journal</u>, "Why does not the <u>Standard</u> ridicule the 'brogue' of Alderman Sheeran! Why he votes as the <u>Standard</u> clique directs him to and Alderman Connolly don't--that makes all the difference."[10] By a variety of means, then, the native-born Democrats worked to control their Irish brethren.

Between 1867 and 1869 the nature of the Board of Aldermen changed rapidly. The board elected in April 1867 consisted of five native-born Republicans, five native-born Democrats, and four Irish Democrats. Two years later, while the party ratio remained unchanged, the ethnic complexion of both parties was much different. The number of Irish Democrats had grown from four to six, and the Republicans now consisted of one native-born, two Germans and two Britons (see Table XXIV). Although no longer drawn from the city's elite, the new aldermen nevertheless still remained in many ways deferential to the old elite after 1867. The Irish Democrats on the board followed the lead of the native-born in filling the city's appointive offices. Each year they elected former Know-Nothings as

TABLE XXIV

JERSEY CITY ALDERMEN BY ETHNICITY, 1857, 1867, 1869

	1857		1867		1869	
	N	%	N	%	N	%
Native-born	13	81.3	10	71.4	4	28.6
Irish	3	18.7	4	28.6	6	42.8
German	0	0.0	0	0.0	2	14.3
British	0	0.0	0	0.0	2	14.3
TOTAL	16	100.0%	14	100.0%	14	100.0%

City Marshall, Collector of Revenue, and Treasurer, and native-born Democrats as Controller, City Clerk, and City Attorney. Had Irish aldermen attempted to run Irish candidates for these important offices, Republicans probably would have voted for native-born Democrats rather than see these offices filled with Irish appointees.[11]

This transition did not go unnoticed. The Evening Journal noted in 1868 that "old Know Nothing Democrats" had, until recently, "been smart enough to honeyfugle the Irish into doing all the heavy voting and yelling while they took all the fat offices themselves." But now "Pat has worked up to a conscious sense of his power, and demands the offices himself."[12] When the aldermen selected an Irishman to succeed a deceased native-born Democrat as one of the three water commissioners, the Journal claimed that "the intelligent citizens of Jersey City" would not "submit to this sort of thing" for long. "This Irish element in our community," the <u>Journal</u> continued, "puts upon us three-fourths of all the taxes arising from pauperism, intemperance and crime, does three-fourths of all the bogus voting and then rules the city--by sheer force of numbers and the help of another class of citizens who ought to know better."[13] Here was the problem facing the old elite stated in succinct terms: how to contain a culturally different majority.

Contemptuous of immigrants in power, the <u>Journal</u> sent a reporter to a meeting of "THAT KOMMON KOUNCIL" in October 1868:

> Taint often I go tu that air place; aint bin thar since they played "seven aitch."* I heered they war agoin to eleck Jugges and Klerks fur the cumin elekshion so I thought as it war a leetle out of the reglar rutine of bussness that I wud go. The fust thing I noticed was Lehon Habbitt, Cheef of Polise Phowler and Kommissuner Pray a torking with all of the Bord on Sumthink wich peered tu me tu meen sumthink strickly konfidenshul of course.

The meeting allegedly continued with absurdity piled on absurdity:

> I mentally suggested that the President ought tu

---

*The aldermen elected in April 1868 took from May to July to effect an organization, with "seven aitch" the recorded vote on hundreds of ballots as the Democrats deadlocked on whether to elect Hosea Clark or William Clarke as their president. <u>Jersey City Times</u>, May 1 - July 8, 1868, <u>passim</u>.

> have made a motion for a recess, for 6 months,
> so that the oneddicated part of the kouncil kud
> hev the advantages of the Primary Skool. That
> wasn't the wust of it, Goorman got elekted, as
> John Gourman and was declared elckted, wen Ald
> Shearon, no relation to Shearon Springs, stated
> that he had furgotten the english in Gorman's
> name, and begged leave to hev a <u>haitch</u> inserted
> <u>atwixt</u> the John and the Gorman making it John
> H. Gorman. Ald Kirsten said he woodent have it
> put in, and thus the row wen on, an on, and I
> went on--tu the door, I felt as how I coodnt
> set with such an intellectooal crowd, who seemed
> tu be trying wich cood waste the most time.[14]

Here was vivid recognition of both the class and ethnic shift in who served as aldermen after 1867. While Democrats continued to control the Board and Irish Democrats deferred to native Democrats on appointments, aldermen responded to social issues in ways more sympathetic to the city's poor. A machinists' strike against the Erie in early 1870, for example, received official treatment quite unlike the tunnel laborers' strike in 1859. When the Erie machinists left their jobs in the huge repair shops adjacent to the Long Dock on January 12, 1870, the issue was similar to that of the tunnelmen's strike in 1859. The twelfth had been pay day, but the men had not been paid. Four months earlier, in October 1869, after numerous late payments, Jay Gould and representatives of each repair shop on the line had signed an agreement stipulating a monthly pay day. Jersey City men were to get paid on the twelfth, for example, and Port Jervis men on the twenty-

fifth. From October to December 1869 the men received
their pay on time. But when the 350 Jersey City men were
not paid by 4 p. m. on January 12, 1870, they quit work.
Returning in a body on the following morning, they offered to work only if paid. When told that the paymaster was
regrettably ill, they formally struck.[15]

Although largely Irish, these were not unskilled men.
They consisted largely of machinists, carpenters, boilermakers, and blacksmiths and had a weak union, the Mutual
Protective Association, created originally to deal with
the 1869 difficulties. Both sides saw the central strike
issue as one of industrial discipline. On January 15, the
Erie fired all strikers, and Jay Gould issued a statement
stating that the company would "maintain discipline at any
cost," and demanded protection of company property by
Jersey City police. Two days later, the men issued a public appeal for support, citing the need to impose discipline on the Erie. Implying that the strike had been
forced to break up their organization and repudiate the
1869 agreement, they accused Gould of finding "the dull
times, the inclement season, and the great number of men
out of employment . . . too _Goulden_ an opportunity to be
lost in stamping out the manhood of his victims." If they
allowed Erie to pay them late once, they reasoned, they
would be paid late every month.[16]

Under the leadership of George Keasley, the Mutual Protective Association pursued two policies. The first was to discourage new men from working in the repair shops; the second was a completely unsuccessful attempt to extend the strike to other repair shops along the line. Detailing pickets to watch the ferries from New York and to guard the entrances to the shops, the strikers prevented the Erie from filling their places while maintaining, claimed the generally unsympathetic <u>Journal</u>, "the utmost decorum." The strategy succeeded for ten days, and the shops remained virtually at a standstill. Then the Erie, relying on "New York toughs and Jersey City constables," sought to reopen them in earnest. Recruiting New York and Paterson Germans, the Erie brought them to Jersey City as a group on the twenty-fourth and used the police to march them from the docks to the shops.[17]

That evening the strikers and their families gathered to "salute in their peculiar way" the men recruited by the Erie. Although a platoon of city police escorted the men to the ferries, they made no effort to interfere with the strikers, and, reported the <u>Journal</u>, "allowed themselves to be jostled by the mob and treated with supreme contempt." The police protected the Erie employees, but with little enthusiasm. The following day witnessed a repetition but with more strike-breakers, more police, and a larger crowd.

Although the crowd shouted and threw stones, no one was injured. The *Journal* blamed the "large crowd of women . . . whose threats and epithets were framed in the coarsest and most profane language," for inciting the men to violence. The police prevailed, however, and on the following day, January 26, the strikers admitted defeat and disbanded their organization.[18]

Although the strike had ended, it reverberated in municipal politics for another month. On January 25, after the first scuffle, the aldermen unanimously requested the mayor to use his influence to have the men reinstated, and an ineffectual correspondence between Mayor William Clarke and Jay Gould followed. A week later the aldermen, led by Patrick Sheeran, passed resolutions mildly criticizing the police commissioners for the role they played in the unsuccessful strike. Sheeran supported his resolution with vehemence and in language thoroughly unacceptable to the old elite who had governed the city for so long:

> The Chief of Police marshalled this force of policemen to protect men from New York, who do not pay taxes here, and I as a taxpayer am opposed to anything of the kind. These strikers should be respected and I want to know what business this man Chief Fowler had to take the police force, not one or two nights, but even up to the present time, to protect the property of the Erie Railway Company and prevent a riot. How dare he prevent a row, and keep the New Yorkers from getting licked?[19]

While the Erie Railway Company had never been popular in Jersey City, demanding respect for Irish strikers was quite a new phenomenon in Jersey City's aldermanic chamber. The Journal thought the aldermen "dummies" for "censuring the police for protecting life and property in this city."[20] Sheeran, however, persisted. During the following month he objected to a pay raise for Chief Fowler and finally--a minority of one--opposed the warrant to pay the police for strike duty on the grounds that the railroad, not the city, should pay the bill.[21]

Sheeran's words, "these strikers should be respected," symbolized the change in Jersey City's aldermen. More and more of them came from the same culture as the strikers themselves and knew what it meant to be a working class immigrant in an American city. They showed little sympathy to temperance, to the silent Sabbath, or to the conception of order which demanded quiet acquiescence on the part of the immigrant poor. When the Rev. James Harkness, a Scotland-born Calvinist, told the City Mission and Tract Society that "if we could make the members of our Common Council city missionaries it would be a good thing," he got a good laugh.[22]

The idea, however, was on many minds. If more people responsive to the ideals embodied in the City Mission and Tract Society could be brought into Jersey City, perhaps control of the city would revert to those who had held it for so long. For this reason events soon after the strike acquire special significance. Two months later, Jersey City consolidated with the City of Bergen and Hudson City, municipalities respectively southwest and northwest of Jersey City itself. Considered for over a decade, consolidation aimed at unifying the half-dozen towns in Hudson County opposite New York. In a referendum during the fall of 1869, each town voted on whether or not to merge into Jersey City, with the stipulation that the enlarged city would contain only contiguous territory. Union Township, for example, voted to merge, but intervening West Hoboken did not.[23] Only Bergen and Hudson voted yes and were contiguous to Jersey City. Ratified in November 1869, consolidation took effect in May 1870, and Jersey City now included two communities whose development was quite different from that of Jersey City itself.

The larger of the two communities, Hudson City, had been incorporated in 1855 with a population of 3300. Although this had grown to 21,000 by 1870, the city had made little progress in public improvements, and consolidation, it was hoped, would bring sewers and paved streets. Hudson was an immigrant city. A large planned German settlement in 1855 formed the nucleus for a large German community, and the Bergen tunnelmen, introduced at the same time,

MAP I

WARD BOUNDARIES, JERSEY CITY, 1870

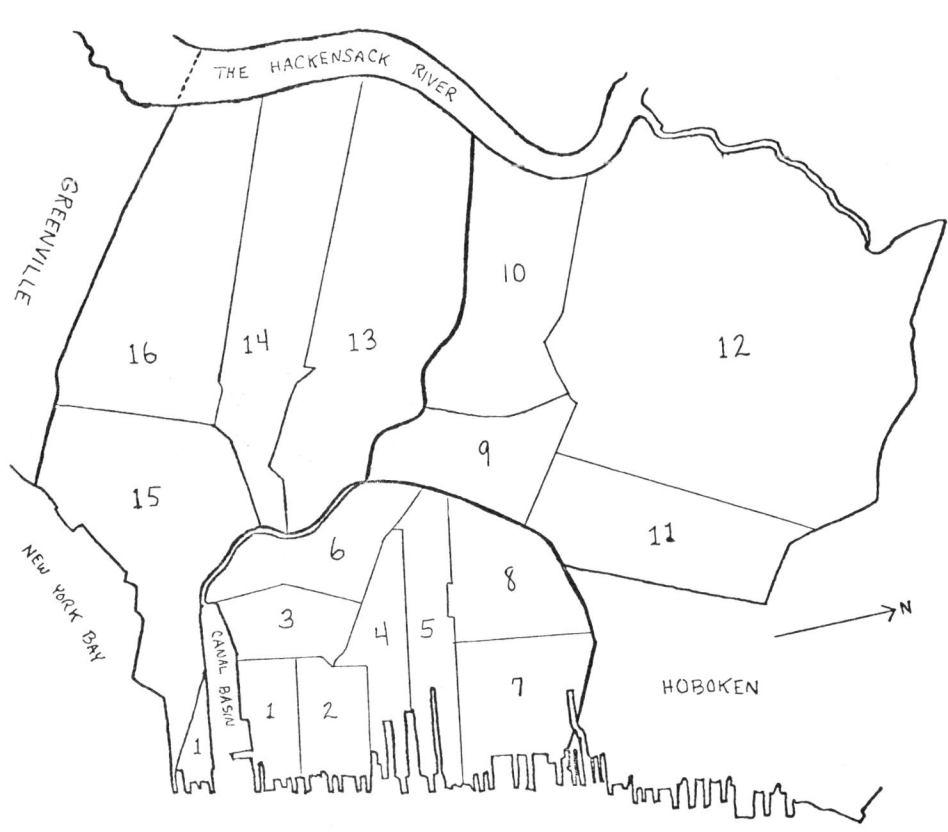

Wards 1 - 8   Jersey City
      9 - 12 Hudson City
      13 - 16 City of Bergen

formed the nucleus of an equally large lower class Irish community.[24] Industry centered in the large stockyards controlled by the railroads and on quarrying the granite in Bergen Hill. The City of Bergen had a much different complexion. Occupying a choice location overlooking New York Bay, Bergen was a middle class suburb of New York and Jersey City with almost no industry and an overwhelmingly native-born population. Many of its 13,600 residents had moved from Jersey City during or after the Civil War. Of the twelve Bergen aldermen elected in 1869, for example, six had been Jersey City residents before 1860, as had been four of the sixteen school board members. As in Hudson, public improvements had not kept pace with population growth, and the city was deeply in debt.[25]

The population make-up of each community influenced its approach to consolidation. The *Evening Journal* claimed that the "respectable" element in neighboring communities would consolidate only reluctantly because of "a ruling voting element here that often selects and forces into office men notoriously the most incompetent and least fit for the responsibilities of official positions."[26] Pangborn of course meant the Irish. In Hudson City, on the other hand, while the Irish reportedly favored consolidation, the Germans, the most influential element, reportedly opposed it. As one Hudson Cityite said at a public meeting, "they would simply be the fag end of Jersey City."[27] This fear of being left a "fag-end" influenced municipal decisions in both Hudson and Bergen between the approval and the fact of consolidation. Both cities voted to begin mammoth street and sewer projects with the burden to fall on the larger city later. Irregularities abounded, and when the Jersey City clerk called at the respective city halls of Hudson and Bergen soon after consolidation, he found that while the contracts remained intact, most other municipal records had been unceremoniously destroyed.[28]

The government of the consolidated city was basically the government of Jersey City writ large. The four Bergen and four Hudson wards were grafted onto the eight of Jersey City. Thirty-two aldermen, two from each ward, held municipal power under the charter voted by the legislature in the spring of 1870. A five-man elected commission ran the police department, and the mayor was little more than a figurehead. Enlarging the city weakened the power of the old Know-Nothing Democrats who had exercised such an important influence for so long. Although Jersey City's elite had seen consolidation as a means of preserving their position in the city, this was not to be the case. In 1870 Jersey City's immigrant population actually became much more influential and the government became much more responsive to immigrant needs.

Held in the three separate cities, the April 1870 municipal election produced the Board of Aldermen who took office on May 1, 1870. According to the always suspicious Journal, the election came off with "less cheating and illegal voting than usual," and the result was "much nearer a real expression of the wishes of the people." The overwhelmingly Democratic victory came from "the 'mighty foine' vote pulled in the Corkonian wards."[29] Of the thirty-two aldermen, twenty-three were Democrats, and nine were Republicans. During the following year each was the subject of a biography in the weekly Jersey City Herald, and from these it is possible to put together a composite portrait of these men.

The Herald was edited by Hugh F. McDermott, an editor unlike any other in Jersey City. Born in 1834 to Protestant parents in Ireland, he was raised as part of the Irish middle class. The family emigrated to Boston when the famine destroyed his father's business. Offered a full scholarship to Brown University on the condition that he become a Presbyterian minister, he refused it and went to San Francisco to edit The Golden Era. Here he employed Bret Harte as a typesetter and wrote a play that he sold for a substantial sum. Returning east in 1857 he participated in New York literary society and in 1864 started a weekly paper in Hudson City. An agnostic, he ridiculed evangelical religion and its embodiment in the Republican party and championed the city's poor. He also supported Irish nationalism and saw Orange Day as the day "a foreign bastard reduced a noble and virtuous people to bondage."[30] The biographies reflected his biases. While including social and economic data, they barely mentioned religious activities.[31]

Eleven aldermen were native-born of native-born parents, and eight of them were part of the city's economic elite. They were commission merchants, stock traders, and contractors. Most were also large real estate holders, ranging up to Horatio N. Ege's $150,000 in local land. The three not in the elite were by no means poor. Isaac Freese, Jr., a young stock-yard superintendent, eventually went into business for himself. The two others were liquor dealers, but both conducted their businesses in New York and commuted daily; they were not mere saloon-keepers. No native-born aldermen were artisans or laborers. Only two were born or raised in Jersey City; the majority came from rural New York or New Jersey and reached Jersey City via business interests in New York. To Jersey City they brought rural values mingled with urban business experience.

Most numerous, the Irish aldermen totaled fourteen of the whole. Eight were first generation, and the rest were the children of immigrants. While about half seem to have owned real estate, only two clearly belonged to the economic elite. John Hogan, who ran his own Hudson City cattle business, owned over $100,000 in real estate, and John Egan employed about thirty men in a carpentry shop and also owned real estate. Only two, however, were workers, both labor leaders. Blacklisted by the Erie for his role in the 1870 machinists' strike, John Maloney had opened a small saloon after election as alderman from the seventh ward, the site of the Erie shops. Francis S. Fitzpatrick was a master machinist and led the Iron and Metal Workers Association in an unsuccessful eight-hour strike in 1872. Both were second generation and had attended James Brann's school at St. Peter's in the 1850's. The other ten Irish aldermen fell between the working class and the elite in Jersey City's social structure. They included grocers, marketmen, two soda water manufacturers, two Erie freight agents, a carriage manufacturer, and a butcher. While most had relatively high-status occupations in the Irish community, they were not high-status in terms of the native-born community. Additionally, most had begun as poor but not destitute men. The career of John Egan was atypical only in that he achieved greater success. Born in County Roscommen in 1824, he was trained as a carpenter, his father's trade. The family emigrated in 1845, and

Egan worked as a carpenter in New York and as a hobbyhorse manufacturer in Brooklyn before beginning his successful Jersey City carpenter's shop. Patrick Harrington's father was a butcher who immigrated in 1848 and brought his family over two years later. Following in his father's footsteps, Harrington ran the family stall in Washington market, New York, and by the time of the 1870 census possessed $4000 in real estate and $600 in personal property. Thus Irish political leadership came from the artisan class. With one possible exception every Irish alderman had begun as a skilled laborer or a small proprietor. Significantly, not only had none ever been an unskilled laborer, but of the nine for whom father's occupation is available, only three came from unskilled households.

Two other influences shaped the lives of Jersey City's Irish aldermen. Although the <u>Herald</u> avoided religion in its biographies, all but one seem to have been Catholic, and several were active in church affairs. Patrick McNulty and Francis S. Fitzpatrick were active in Catholic total abstinence societies, and John Hogan, when a ward school trustee in New York City during the Civil War, had fought successfully to introduce the Douay Bible into the school in his ward. More nebulous in its effect, but important, was the influence of the Irish famine during the 1840's and 1850's. Emigration dates were given for six of the eight Irish-born aldermen. Only one emigrated before the famine; the rest were all part of the famine emigration, and that experience must have left its indelible influence on their minds.

The three British aldermen were of a slightly higher economic status, but all seem to have started poor. Thomas Gross came from Liverpool, emigrating in 1854 with his parents. Although his father was a stevedore in 1860, by 1870 father and son ran a carting concern of some consequence, having contracts with numerous shipping firms. William Bumsted was the son of a Baptist mason who had emigrated in 1836 rather than pay church rates in his native Norfolk. A successful contractor, Bumsted had moved to more affluent Bergen and had served as a Bergen alderman before consolidation. Gaelic-speaking Neil Campbell came from Scotland. Born in 1830, Campbell emigrated with his family in 1842, joining an aged relative in agricultural Orange County, New York. The relative, Campbell told the _Herald_, had been captured by Washington's forces at the battle of Winchester. Joining the Revolutionary Army, he remained in America after the war. Like Bumsted, Campbell, a teetotaler and owner of a large wholesale masonry supplies business, must be considered part of the economic elite. The British-born aldermen greatly resembled the native-born in economic and social position.

Three German proprietors sat on the board, all of them small businessmen. Born in Baden, Tobias Martini had worked in various New York City retail stores until opening a saloon in Hudson City. Having emigrated largely to escape the Prussian draft, he had paid $825 for a substitute during the Civil War. Christopher Tangeman also ran a saloon as well as a grocery. Secretary of the Liquor Dealers Association in 1867, he had publicly opposed Mayor Gopsill's temperance crusade, but did not run for office until 1870. The Herald described him as believing "in the Cavour maxim 'a free church in a free state,' or in other words, he is not a bigot and likes his lager." Anton Schick was a Hudson City grocer who had been trained as a varnisher before emigrating in 1851 to join a brother already in Hudson City. None of the Germans were either working class or wealthy. All three were proprietors, two of them saloon-keepers.

Jersey City's aldermen, then, were divided on class lines similar to the ethnic lines. All but two native-born and two of three Britons were of the economic elite. All but two Irishmen and all three Germans fell into various categories below the elite, as railroad and factory supervisors, grocers and saloon-keepers, and skilled workmen. Most, if not of the working class, had working class roots. Regional differences within the city complicated the class and ethnic picture (see Table XXV). Bergen, for

TABLE XXV

JERSEY CITY ALDERMEN BY ETHNICITY AND AREA, 1870

	Old Jersey City	Hudson	Bergen	TOTAL
Native-born	4	1	6	11
Irish, 1st gen.	5	3	0	8
Irish, 2nd gen.	4	2	1	7
British	2	0	1	3
German	1	2	0	3
TOTAL	16	8	8	32

example, sent eight men, seven of whom were clearly in the economic elite. A largely native-born area, Bergen sent six natives, one upper class Englishman, and a second-generation Irish Protestant, who was not only of the elite, but also was a Methodist Sunday School superintendent. Hudson City, on the other hand, sent seven immigrants and one native. Jersey City contributed four native-born, nine Irish, two British, and a German. With Bergen deleted, the aldermen were only twenty percent native-born.

This body of aldermen further reduced the power of the native-born Democrats who had exercised a disproportionate influence for so long. The first test of this power came in early May when the aldermen chose a corporation printer, a post occupied by John Lyons for a decade. Always elected as a matter of routine, Lyons won this year but only on the second ballot. The roll calls provide insights into divisions within the board and within the society that elected it. Three men were in nomination: Lyons, Z. K. Pangborn, and William D. McGregor, the Irish editor of the <u>Hudson City Gazette</u>. On the first ballot Lyons received the votes of the native-born Democrats and those old Jersey City Irish aldermen who had traditionally supported him, a total of sixteen. Pangborn received nine Republican votes and McGregor the votes of Hudson City Irish Democrats and the Jersey City Irish who had always operated independently of the native-born, a total of seven. As Lyons received exactly half of the thirty-two votes, a second ballot followed. Deserting Pangborn, native-born Republicans joined the Democrats to elect Lyons and defeat McGregor.[32] Here was a pattern that would become familiar: native-born Republicans and Democrats closed ranks when the Irish seemed likely to increase their power in important areas.

In other offices native-born Democrats did less well. Bernard McGuigan, reputedly the first child born in Jersey City to Irish Catholic parents, replaced Know-Nothing Samuel D. Ellis as city marshall.[33] Similarly, David Hallanan replaced Edward F. C. Young as treasurer, and Samuel McBurney replaced Thomas Benwell as comptroller. The important offices that dealt with taxation and finance were falling into Irish hands.[34]

The school board nominations submitted by Mayor Charles H. O'Neill in June 1870 created more controversy. Designed to parallel the Board of Aldermen, the school board included thirty-two men, two from each ward, elected by the aldermen. O'Neill's list was heavily weighted toward the old native-born elite with no more than a third Irish and at least six ex-Know-Nothings, including John Lyons. After a month of juggling names, the aldermen scrapped O'Neill's list completely and agreed that each would nominate one man who would be confirmed by the rest. The school board, as it finally emerged, resembled the Board of Aldermen in its ethnic and religious complexion: almost half appear to have been Irish Catholics, a fact that did not set well with the Evening Journal.[35]

Immigrant aldermen appointing immigrants to high offices and pursuing policies of benefit to the immigrant communities was not what the Journal had anticipated from consolidation of the three cities. Through the summer of 1870 the Journal kept up a steady attack on these men: they were certainly extravagant, probably corrupt, and definitely unfit. The issue seized upon as symbolic proof of both corruption and incompetence was the salary the aldermen voted themselves in July 1870. Meeting two afternoons a week and often far into the night, Jersey City's aldermen spent long hours on city business. There was much to do in integrating the three separate municipalities whose roads, sewers, and water distribution systems had not been built with connection in mind. Additionally, the contracts let by Bergen and Hudson immediately before consolidation created a large debt that required funding. Believing themselves deserving, the aldermen voted themselves a twelve hundred dollar annual salary although the city charter was silent on the subject.[36] A number of native-born citizens, led by Dudley S. Gregory, the city's richest man, petitioned the courts to void the salary on the grounds that the charter did not provide for it. While the *Journal* attacked the salary as a raid on the treasury, the *Jersey City Herald* supported it. Noting that few men could provide services for nothing, the *Herald* correctly saw in this issue a struggle for control of the city between its wealthy native-born and the immigrant poor. "Dudley S. Gregory is a good citizen--so they say," wrote McDermott. "Dudley is rich, and is therefore an honest man." But would he work for nothing? McDermott thought not. He then justified the salary as required not only by the nature of the work, but also by the circumstances of the aldermen:

> The majority of our Aldermen are active, intelligent hardworking artisans who are among the bone and sinew of our city. These men are poor, and certainly cannot, in justice to themselves and

> those dependent upon them for support, afford to leave their employment whenever called upon without compensation.[37]

The people, thought the <u>Herald</u>, would support the salary for the same reasons they supported the aldermen. The salary did not stand, however; the State Supreme Court ruled in March 1871 that as the charter prohibited aldermen from holding any paying city job, the office of alderman could not be made a paying city job. "Honest" Dudley, member of the Erie Railroad board of directors, triumphed.[38]

Gregory did succeed in uncovering one case of official corruption later in the year. When the city bought property on the Hackensack River for a municipal dock, the price seemed rather high. Inquiring further, Gregory found that two aldermen were interested parties, and on his own initiative, he had the sale voided in the courts. The aldermen involved, however, were atypical. British-born William Bumsted was worth over a hundred thousand dollars, and native-born William Van Keuran was worth slightly less. Both were street contractors and involved with the pre-consolidation Bergen street and sewer contracts. Meanwhile, the <u>Journal</u> thundered against the incompetence of immigrant artisans in high places.[39]

The aldermen responded to the aspirations of their immigrant constituents in a number of ways. One was through their support of Irish nationalist activity. When Jeremiah O'Donovan Rossa and a group of Irish nationalists exiled by the British visited New York, the aldermen attempted to make them official guests of the city. Noting that America "has ever been an asylum to the oppressed of all despotic governments," and the exiles "have been banished from their country by the tyrant who has held that country in chains for centuries," the aldermen resolved, under Patrick Harrington's leadership, to appropriate five hundred dollars for an official celebration. Again aroused, native-born taxpayers threatened court action, and the aldermen rescinded the appropriation. The reception was held anyway, but as a private rather than as a public reception.[40]

Irish nationalists were more successful in gaining use of the city armory for drill. Used only by the national guard, the armory had been sought by, but denied to, Irish drill companies for years. After national guardsmen got into a brawl while attending the funeral of General Edwin R. V. Wright, the aldermen decided to end this exclusivity and grant drill privileges to the Emmett Guards.[41] Soon after, the Slievenamon Guards received the same privilege, a move opposed by Pangborn and the Journal. Calling Pangborn's comments "vituperations," John Boyde, Slievenamon Centre, justified armory use.

Besides working for "liberation of Ireland from the accursed British yoke," he claimed, the Guards were working for the protection and preservation of liberty generally. In this respect they were as "American" as the national guard itself.[42]

While the 1870 aldermen responded to the city's immigrant population more directly than any previous board, in certain important ways they deferred to the old Know-Nothing leadership. John Lyons continued as city printer although his paper was as anti-Irish as ever. Jeremiah Cleveland, Orestes' brother and an O. A. U. leader in the 1850's, remained a favored street contractor.[43] Native-born Democrats held most elective offices above the local level, such as state assemblymen and state senator. Party machinery above the ward level remained a tenuous native-born preserve. Even this power was challenged in the fall of 1870 when the middle class Irish rebelled at what they saw as an unholy alliance between rich Know-Nothings and poor Irish. Although this rebellion failed, it brought together native-born Republicans and Democrats who successfully petitioned the 1871 legislature to end immigrant influence in Jersey City by having the state legislature itself appoint local officials in Jersey City. Discussed in the next two chapters, the attempt by the Irish to operate independently of the native-born Democratic elite led directly to a six-year abolition of local government in Jersey City.

DOCUMENTATION: CHAPTER V

[1] The "Junius" letters appeared in the Jersey City Chronicle, between April 1 and 4, 1863.

[2] Ibid.

[3] Ibid., April 15, 1863.

[4] Newark Daily Advertiser, October 5, 6, 8, 1866.

[5] Standard, December 15, 17, 1864.

[6] Ibid., April 11, 1868.

[7] New York Herald, November 10, 1870; Journal, November 1, 1870.

[8] Journal, October 13, 1870.

[9] Jersey City Times, April 11, 1871.

[10] Journal, May 25, 1867. This was followed with the usual charge that "the Standard holds on to the fat treasury teat, at which it has so long been sucking, only by the votes of Irishmen."

[11] New York Tribune, May 7, 1867, May 4, 1869.

[12] Journal, November 20, 1868.

[13] Ibid., December 2, 1868. The deceased water commissioner, Jacob R. Wortendryhe, had first been elected in 1856 with Know-Nothing support and was prominently associated with the City Mission and Tract Society. Ibid., November 7, 1868; New York Tribune, April 3, 1856.

[14] Journal, October 21, 1868.

[15] Ibid., January 13, 1870; New York Times, January 14, March 31, 1871.

[16] Journal, January 15, 17, 1870; New York Tribune, January 18, 1870.

[17] Journal, January 25, 26, 1870; New York Tribune, January 25, 26, 1870.

[18] Journal, January 28, 1870.

[19] Ibid., February 2, 1870.

[20] Ibid.

[21] Ibid., February 16, March 2, 1870.

[22] Ibid., December 9, 1867.

[23] New York Times, March 16, 1868; McLean, p. 80.

[24] McLean, pp. 67-69; Charles H. Winfield, History of the County of Hudson, New Jersey (New York, 1874), p. 324; Standard, October 18, 1866.

[25] McLean, pp. 76-78; Journal, February 24, 1870.

[26] Journal, December 12, 1868.

[27] Ibid., January 6, 1869.

[28] McLean, pp. 78-81.

[29] Journal, April 11, 1870.

[30] New York Times and New York Tribune, June 5, 1890; Journal, June 6, 1890; Jersey City Herald, July 23, 1870.

[31] The biographies appeared in the Jersey City Herald from July 30, 1870, to February 25, 1871. Shorter accounts appeared in the Jersey City Times, May 10, 1870.

[32] Manual of the Board of Aldermen of Jersey City, 1870-1871 (Jersey City, 1871), p. 40 (hereafter cited as Manual ... 1870-1871).

[33] McLean, p. 97; on McGuigan, see Irish World, June 7, 1873.

[34] McLean, pp. 97, 100.

[35] Manual ... 1870-1871, pp. 43-44 95-96; Journal, July 13, 1870. Most school board members, except those from the native-born elite, had no previous political experience.

[36] Journal, June 14, 1870. Although Mayor O'Neill vetoed the salary, the aldermen passed it over his veto. Ibid., June 15, 22, 1870.

[37] Jersey City Herald, July 2, 1870.

[38] New York Times, March 3, 1871. Gregory was also a leading director of the New Jersey Railroad, and a financial angel for both Z. K. Pangborn and Horace Greeley. Journal, December 9, 1874; Glyndon Van Deusen, Horace Greeley: Nineteenth Century Crusader (New York, 1953), pp. 37, 51.

[39] Jersey City Gazette, March 4, 1871; Jersey City Herald, April 15, 1871; Journal, January 25, 1871.

[40] Manual . . . 1870-1871, p. 258; New York Times, February 22, 1871.

[41] New York Times, January 20, 26, 1871; New York Tribune, January 23, 1870. Wright was popular with Hudson County's Irish. Mayor of Hudson City in 1855, he had earned Irish trust and was chosen by the tunnel strikers in 1859 to act as arbitrator with the railroads.

[42] Journal, March 8, 1871; Standard, March 10, 1871.

[43] Jeremiah Cleveland was a Jersey City alderman from 1853 to 1855. Moving to Bergen between 1860 and 1863, he served as a Bergen school director from 1864 to 1867 and as an alderman in 1868. With a financial interest in the American Standard and with his brother the Jersey City Democratic leader, he remained an important figure in Jersey City politics. In 1870 he was the exclusive agent for Nicholson pavement, a process using specially treated wood blocks. Although not considered long-lasting, it was adopted by the aldermen for many streets. McLean, p. 78; Shaw, p. 1142; Journal, November 1, 1870.

CHAPTER VI

THE LACE CURTAIN REVOLT

On a spring day in 1861 a <u>New York World</u> reporter contemplated a switch tender at a downtown New York street railway intersection. The man would come out of a small shelter on the sidewalk every few minutes and throw a switch for a Sixth Avenue car, then throw it back to direct a car up Eighth Avenue. "What a bleak prospect really lies before him," thought the reporter, "switchman today, switchman tomorrow, switchman may be until the day he dies." The reporter turned to the switchman's larger significance: "He will die one of these days; who will bury him? Who will miss him?" No one, he thought, no one at all; certainly not the company or passengers and maybe not his wife and children. Contemplation led him to reconstruct the switchman's past:

> Years ago the poor fellow had hopes, high, boyish hopes. He had heard of America, in his humble Irish hut; he was told that work was plenty here; that wages were high; that he could soon climb the ladder of respectability and rank, and make a man of himself, all of which he knew well enough he could not do in the old country. So he bid farewell to his friends, kissed his blue-eyed Kathleen, and bade her dry her tears, for he would write as soon as he reached New York, and after a little while send passage money to bring her over too.

He worked on the streets and on the railroads, brought

Kathleen over, married her, and settled down to raise a family on the same wages he had received when single.

> Poor fellow! What a life he has led ever since! A battle with poverty, a race with death. And don't you think that he feels it all, as with downcast eye and sullen mien he performs his irksome task on the track? Don't you think that his proud Irish heart beats madly under his well worn coat when he feels that his old hopes are dashed to the ground, that his darling Kathleen's love has been wasted on him, that his child were better dead than living. Perhaps he does. But for all that he turns the switch once more! Poor fellow![1]

Here was a central truth of the Irish experience in mid-nineteenth century urban America. Unskilled labor wrestled in unfair combat with the American dream and lost, a fair proportion of the time. Mobility out of the working class was difficult enough for the native-born Protestant; for the Irish Catholic the barriers to affluence were even greater. Some, of course, did make it. With greater talent, harder work, and more luck, a small number rose into the economic elite as merchants, brokers and manufacturers. They had gained but half the switchman's dream, however, for rank and respectability did not necessarily follow affluence. Irish Catholic merchants did not lose the stigma of Catholicism when they attempted to enter the world of the native-born elite.[2]

By 1870 Jersey City had a comparatively large Irish middle class. Many had prospered in New York City, and like their native-born counterparts had moved to Jersey

City and now took the ferries to their shops and businesses each day. They played a minor role, however, in the life of the city. Excluded both politically and socially, they were acutely aware that affluence had not brought status outside the Irish community. In 1870 a movement among the city's "respectable" Irish attempted to oust the old Know-Nothing leadership in the local Democratic party and to gain the influence they had assumed their position would bring. Organized as the Young Democrats, they sought to prevent the re-election of former Mayor Orestes Cleveland to Congress and to elect an Irish assembly slate that would be independent of the traditional native-born leadership. When this failed, one of the more active Young Democrats became the recognized force in the Catholic Total Abstinence Union, a movement of largely middle class Irish Catholics to find respectability in a society that allowed them opportunity but not recognition. The Young Democrats and the Catholic Total Abstinence Union provide insights into the frustrations and hopes of the new middle class Irish, how they related to their Irish heritage, and how they interacted with their much more numerous "shanty" Irish neighbors.

The Young Democrat movement in 1870 revolved around the congressional nomination of Orestes Cleveland for a second term. A Know-Nothing from 1856 to 1859 and mayor from 1863 to 1866, Cleveland was sent to Congress in 1868, nominated by a divided convention and elected by a narrow margin.[3] A large number of delegates of the September 1870 nominating convention walked out on the the grounds that the convention was packed for Cleveland, and even after their departure the convention leaders had their problems. Cleveland's nomination "was responded to by such a storm of shouts, groans and hisses that the convention came to an abrupt termination."[4] The seceders, meanwhile, met in a Hoboken hotel and arranged for a separate convention.

Meeting one week later, the Young Democrats, under the leadership of Frederick W. Wolbert, a native-born Catholic, nominated Aeneas Fitzpatrick, a forty-year-old Irish Catholic merchant. Moving to Jersey City, probably from New York, during the Civil War, Fitzpatrick dealt in wholesale crockery from offices in New York and lived in what a New York Sun reporter called "a plain comfortable mansion" in one of the city's more elite areas. In his acceptance speech, he railed against "party hacks" and urged the election of "honest men" to office, even if it were necessary "to descend to the ranks of the workingmen to find honest men."[5] This was not the first time that Fitzpatrick had bolted from the Democratic party. Failing to gain the Democratic nomination for water commissioner in 1869, he first sought the Republican nomination and then ran unsuccessfully as an independent.[6]

Fitzpatrick was fully aware of Irish problems in urban America. Earlier in 1870 he had helped organize the Irish Immigrant Aid and Land Colonization Society, dedicated to helping former Irish peasants begin an agricultural life on American soil. As the principal speaker at the founding meeting he addressed himself to the problems of "young, healthy, robust men" fresh "from the beautiful hills and valleys of Ireland" but forced "to crowd themselves into shanties and tenement houses, where the atmosphere reeks of the foulest odors--an atmosphere pregnant with misery, disease, sickness and death." Of what use, he asked, were "liberty, free government and all that" when a man

> has to work for a mere pittance to purchase diseased meat and the coarsest kind of food, day after day, at some menial service, which by degrees blunts his native instincts, sours his disposition, and degrades him morally and mentally[?][7]

The Irish plight began with distress in Ireland and ended with the social and economic realities of urban America. A social conservative at heart, Fitzpatrick urged successful "experienced" Irishmen to help finance a return to the soil for their poorer countrymen. In doing so he provided insights into his own conception of urban America and how

Irishmen were exploited by native-born citizens. This became, in a manner devoid of political radicalism, a major part of his campaign rhetoric.

The revolt against the native-born Democratic leadership continued through September and October. In the third assembly district Alderman John Meehan organized a "People's Party" after his independent eighth ward delegation was ejected from the nominating convention. Convening on October 12, Meehan's convention nominated Michael Connolly, the independent-minded 1867 alderman whose comments the Standard had reported in brogue. Although Connolly was a substantial contractor, the anti-Irish Journal reported that the convention had nominated "a bricklayer" for the state assembly.[8] The convention also passed resolutions opposing the tax-exempt status of railroads and the "ring" police commission. "Scenes of violence . . . abetted by the police" were common at primaries, they noted, and "when old residents are hauled from primaries like dogs by uniformed partisans," the primaries must be replaced by independent action at the polls.[9]

Following Cleveland's renomination for Congress, the regular Democrats met to nominate candidates for state and county offices. Dominated by native-born Democrats, the county convention selected candidates either native-born or long associated with subservience to native dictates. The nomination for sheriff was especially galling to the Irish. Hudson City Alderman Patrick Harrington had received the nomination in 1869, but, as a result of native-born defections, was the only Democrat on the ticket to fail of election. Desirous of the nomination again in 1870, he was passed over in favor of Thomas Gaffney, an 1868 police commissioner. When a Jersey City alderman in 1866, Gaffney had reportedly suggested that the aldermen respond to a Fenian invitation by accepting, and then attending the meeting armed with broomsticks. Insulted and ignored, Harrington readily accepted the Young Democrats' nomination for sheriff.[10]

The men who organized the Young Democrats were not poor men. Fitzpatrick, Connolly and Harrington were all men of at least moderate substance. Their two most important orators were James Brann, an educator who had been active in Irish and Catholic activities at least since 1857, and John Ignatius Cullen, editor of the Catholic New York Tablet. The Newark Daily Advertiser, a Republican paper that gave much attention to Fitzpatrick, observed at a meeting in October that "It was noticeable . . . that it combined more of the orderly, intelligent and respectable element of the democracy than has been seen in this campaign at any meeting."[11] On the other hand, the Journal described a regular Democratic meeting as "a large number of Irishmen, reeking in filth and stinking liquor, and spoiling for a fight. . . ."[12]

Aware of this difference themselves, the Young Democrats worked to arouse a consciousness of political exploitation among Irish Democrats to split them from the native-born regulars. Early in the campaign, James Brann issued a circular that emphasized Orestes Cleveland's Know-Nothing past and his subsequent slights to the Irish. Brann reminded his audience that, when mayor, Cleveland had promised to preside at a Fenian meeting in Aeneas Fitzpatrick's warehouse, but his "Know Nothing proclivities got the better of him" and although in the city, he stayed away. As a Congressman, Cleveland had shown the same contempt for Cuban independence as he had shown previously for the Irish. "Such a friend of monarchy is unfit to represent free men," he continued, "and he should go to Russia or Japan where he would find more congenial institutions." Brann concluded with an appeal to Irish nationalism. "Let us arise as one man on the morning of election and rebuke the truckling sycophants," he urged. "The vindication of your race from insult demands it, and you may rest assured that every vote given for Cleveland is nothing more or less than an additional rivet in the chains of our brothers suffering in British dungeons."[13]

But the Young Democrats faced a central problem: to bring these issues home to the working class Irish who constituted the bulk of the Democratic electorate. Could the largely symbolic issues of status and recognition that activated the Young Democrats drive a wedge between the native-born elite and the Irish mass? While dominated by nativists, the Democratic organization did provide patronage if not power, and in a lower class community the former probably carried more weight than the latter. Additionally, the Democratic split made a Republican victory likely. Patrick O'Beirne, a middle class Irishman associated with Fitzpatrick in the Irish Immigrant Aid and Land Colonization Society, addressed himself to this problem. Claiming friendship with many Young Democrats, and admitting that the party primaries were "a standing disgrace with us," he nonetheless urged support for Cleveland and the regular Assembly slate on the grounds that to do less would result in a Republican victory. O'Beirne then described the Republican party as more of a threat to Irish aspirations and dignity than the native-born Democrats:

> I cannot forget that within the Radical party at this moment is gathered all the essences of bigotry, intolerance, and proscription for which the old Know Nothing party became, at one and the same time, notorious and odious, and who would proscribe me and my race, and deny us, if they could, the liberties accorded even to the negro.[14]

The editor of the _American Standard_ appended to O'Beirne's letter the names of five Catholic aldermen supporting

Cleveland.

A group of local Fenians approached the issue of possible Republican proscription of Irishmen much more directly. Noting that dissatisfaction with the 1870 aldermen had sparked discussion among Republicans of a plan to abolish local government and substitute state-appointed commissions for all aspects of city administration, they addressed themselves to the important problem of steady employment for unskilled laborers:

> What do we gain if we vote for the Independent Assembly candidates and elect a Republican Assembly, and they commission the Police, Water and other Public Departments of the city, laying out hundreds of Irishmen now in their employ, and Irishmen cannot handle a policeman's club, nor any other official badge for ten years? What do we gain?[15]

No matter what the state of the Democratic party, a Republican victory could only be worse. Noting that there were no Irishmen on the Republican ticket, Hugh McDermott complained in the Jersey City Herald, "What a pitiable sight! Irishmen fighting Irishmen!"[16] In answer, Patrick E. O'Brien, Jersey City's New York Herald correspondent, also a Young Democrat, claimed that "the feeling among the Young Democrats is so intense that they would prefer Republican rule to the present state of things."[17] Fitzpatrick addressed himself to the same issue: "The people are in the hands of a merciless ring," he declaimed at a public meeting, "and /Leon/ Abbett says it himself, but he says reform inside the party, but there is no more chance for this than to institute reform in the infernal regions."[18]

Money again allegedly played its role in binding poor Irish to wealthy native-born. "They debauch young men," claimed Fitzpatrick, "and give them money and make them the tools of politicians."[19] A Fitzpatrick meeting in Newark was almost broken up when "fifty dirty-faced fellows distributed through the hall" "shouted, cheered, laughed and barked" through half a dozen speeches. They were, claimed the orators, from Jersey City and funded by Orestes Cleveland.[20]

While Fitzpatrick railed against Cleveland and the American Standard ("a brainless sheet . . . which has grown rich and opulent off the people"), Cleveland campaigned against the introduction of Chinese labor into the United States, a tactic in which he attempted to include all white labor under a nativistic banner. Coolie labor, wrote Cleveland, would mean first "degradation and ruin" for white workingmen, and finally "the entire degradation of all civilized mechanics." The Newark Daily Advertiser quite correctly interpreted this as a mere extension of Cleveland's former public views on the Irish.[21] The Republican nominee, George A. Halsey, a wealthy Newark leather manufacturer and Congressman from 1866 to 1868, did not mount a vigorous campaign. Confident of victory as Democrats quarreled and divided, Republicans gave as much publicity to Fitzpatrick as to Halsey. Halsey was well known and votes for either would help send a Republican to Washington.[22]

The assembly races attracted as much attention as the congressional campaign. Contesting six assembly seats, Hudson County's Republican ticket consisted of six men in or associated with the business elite. The regular Democratic slate contained a native-born candidate, a German (a 480-pound Hoboken hotel keeper), and four Irishmen, a fact that troubled the Evening Journal. The Irish on the ticket, however, were men basically acceptable to the old native-born Democratic elite. Aldermen Patrick Sheeran and John Whalen, for example, had displayed some independence on social issues but had always voted for the American Standard as city printer and had kept Jeremiah Cleveland, Orestes' brother, busy with street contracts. It was against these men that the Young Democrats ran candidates, nominating men such as Michael Connolly who had been conspicuously independent in local politics or men to whom politics was a new experience.[23]

The election, however, resulted in a Republican victory at all levels and a crushing defeat for the Young

Democrats. Fitzpatrick received just over one percent in the congressional race, receiving no more than ten percent in any Jersey City ward. These were Irish wards, usually heavily Democratic. Not only did Fitzpatrick do best here, but Halsey ran better than Republicans usually did, indicating that not all anti-Cleveland sentiment went to Fitzpatrick. The <u>Jersey City Herald</u> claimed that many Democrats who opposed Cleveland voted for Halsey rather than Fitzpatrick to ensure Cleveland's defeat.[24] The assembly races were only slightly more successful. Michael Connolly, the most articulate and promising candidate, died a week before the election. (Dr. O'Callahan treated him for stomach cramps with an overdose of morphine "which threw him into a slumber from which he never awoke.")[25] With one exception, every race contested by the Young Democrats went to the Republicans, the total anti-Republican vote everywhere a majority. While the Young Democrats won nothing, they did spoil a regular Democratic victory and in one district received twenty-nine percent of the vote.[26]

In the final analysis, however, this independent Irish movement failed to attract a significant number of Irish voters away from traditional voting patterns. Cleveland received 46.7% of the Jersey City vote, and 75% in the largely Irish seventh and eighth wards. Middle class Irishmen were unsuccessful in gaining the allegiance of their working class compatriots. Why would Irishmen, when offered an alternative to the nominees of a party led, as James Brann put it, by "men who were Know Nothings or [are] of notorious anti-Irish proclivities," refuse it? The answers are as complex as they are obscure. The manner in which low-level Irish Democratic leaders related to their neighborhoods is crucial here, but largely unfathomable. The Irish nominated for the assembly seats were certainly well known in their wards and proven vote-getters. Did it really matter, we may therefore ask, if a congressman was a Know-Nothing, as long as one could count on sympathy and support from an alderman or assembly representative? The manner in which the Fenians expressed support for the regular Democrats is suggestive. Noting that a Democratic split would only produce a Republican victory, they connected regular Democratic primacy with Irish public employment, an incontrovertible fact. The Republican victory did, in fact, lead to a wholesale removal of Irishmen (see Chapter VII). Moreover, Fitzpatrick himself talked like a middle class property owner, calling Cleveland "the chief Fugleman, that is to say the William M. Tweed of Hudson County. . . . He is the prime mover in every measure that is calculated to increase our taxes and add to our burden." Fitzpatrick explained that by this he meant that

Cleveland used his influence to get large street contracts for his brother.[27] In all probability, however, only the railroads employed more Irish laborers than the street contractors, and while a small number of Irish complained of high property taxes, a larger number saw in those taxes the opportunity for a dollar a day and perhaps a bit more at election time.[28]

Yet another question revolves about the roots that these middle class men had in the Irish community. None seem to have been active in Irish nationalist circles, although most were prominent in religious activities. Fitzpatrick, for example, was on the Board of Visitors of St. Peter's school, and both James Brann and Michael Connolly had brothers who were local priests.[29] The Irishmen on the Board of Aldermen in 1870 may have been in many ways subservient to the native-born elite, but seemed closer to the working class Irish than the Young Democrats and more acceptable as leaders. Here then was the cruel position of the Young Democrats: ignored by the native-born elite who condemned them for their ethnicity and religion, they also were distrusted by the lower class Irish community, perhaps because their "respectability" made them assume they were the community's leaders. This distrust was not without merit. When the native-born elite recaptured the city in 1871, the Fitzpatrick forces, citing their new class affiliation and ignoring their ethnicity, unsuccessfully sought an alliance.[30]

Defeated at the polls, the Young Democrats in no way ended their quest for respectability in a hostile environment. One Young Democrat threw himself into the Catholic temperance movement and became the driving force in the Catholic Total Abstinence Union of America, an association that very clearly hoped to change the Irish image in the larger society. Hardly a new phenomenon, Catholic temperance in America had begun in the 1830's and culminated with the visit of Father Theobald Mathew in 1849. Depression and war in the 1850's and 1860's left the movement in disarray, and not until after the Civil War did Irish Catholics again form local temperance societies.[31] In 1871 a Jersey City Young Democrat, James W. O'Brien, was the moving force in creating a New Jersey union of local societies, and a year after, the Catholic Total Abstinence Union of America. A study of the society's formation and early years reveals much about the place and thoughts of the middle class Irish in Jersey City.[32]

James W. O'Brien arrived in Jersey City sometime between 1860 and 1866. The owner of a wholesale stationers and job printing establishment in New York, he married Sarah Kelly, the daughter of a retired Jersey City gardener who claimed over twenty thousand dollars worth of real estate in both the 1860 and 1870 census. In 1870 James and Sarah O'Brien and their two children lived with her parents in Jersey City's eighth ward. O'Brien claimed a thousand dollars in personal property and employed one of Sarah's younger brothers as a clerk in his New York business.[33] Twenty-seven years old, he was well aware of the nuances in Jersey City politics. In April 1868, his letter to the New York Sun defended Charles O'Neill as mayoralty candidate, blaming his 1867 defeat on the "defection of ex-Know-Nothings high in the party." He sent an almost identical letter to the American Standard, but with the references to Know-Nothings deleted. When Pangborn, in the Evening Journal, claimed that the Standard had received the same letter as the Sun, and doctored it, O'Brien responded through the Standard. He had written two letters, he claimed, each with a purpose, and denounced Pangborn for his "malicious, illiberal and impertinent" anti-Catholicism.[34]

Later that summer, he probed American politics on a more general level in a letter to the Irish American whose editor, Patrick Meehan, also lived in Jersey City. Addressing himself to the problem of orienting American foreign policy "in favor of the freedom of Ireland," he blamed Irish unquestioning allegiance to the Democratic party for the lack of Irish influence on national policy. "It has been said that on the one side there are no fears and on the other no hopes," he wrote, "and that this necessarily takes the Irish voting power as an item of consideration out of all party councils." Only when the Irish delivered votes to candidates who explicitly addressed themselves to the larger Irish issues, he reasoned, would these issues receive political recognition.[35]

O'Brien, then, approached American politics with a certain sophistication that recognized the need for an independent Irish political consciousness in America. Probably active in eighth ward politics, he was nominated for the school board by Mayor O'Neill in April 1870, but did not receive the approval of the eighth ward aldermen. Later that year he helped organize the Young Democrats in the eighth ward and spoke at a number of ward political gatherings, although not at larger meetings. The Journal noted on one occasion that he "delivered a very fine address" in support of one of the assembly candidates.[36] Already active in St. Michael's Total Abstinence Benevolent Society, he was part of a committee in early 1871 to present resolutions of support to O'Donovan Rossa and his group of exiled Irish patriots.[37]

In 1871, then, O'Brien was a middle class Irishman who had shown his awareness of the fundamental dichotomy in Jersey City's Democratic party and had taken part in an unsuccessful political movement that sought to substitute Irish for native-born leadership. He was also vitally concerned with Irish nationalism and had already taken the temperance pledge. As a temperance leader he would argue that Catholic temperance would not only bring respectability in America, but hasten home rule in Ireland. O'Brien's experience in Jersey City between 1867 and 1871 is crucial to understanding his role in the C. T. A. U.

By 1871 each of Jersey City's Catholic churches had a small temperance society. During the late spring, representatives from each society met to discuss creating a union of all the societies in New Jersey, and under O'Brien's leadership this group created the New Jersey Catholic Total Abstinence Union. The union, they claimed, allowed members of one society to transfer into another without new tests or initiation expenses. "The need for this--in the case of mechanics and working people, who are frequently compelled to move their residence from one locality to another--is clear," reported the committee. "Such members frequently drop out, not being acquainted with the neighborhood."[38] The New Jersey Catholic Total Abstinence Union began in August with six societies, all in Hudson County. By October nineteen others from around the state had joined, and more affiliated over the next few months. Although preceded by state unions in Massachusetts, Connecticut and Rhode Island, the

New Jersey union, with O'Brien as President, quickly became the most prominent and the most aggressive in forming a national union.[39]

Immediately after the state union's formation, O'Brien began a correspondence with other state and local temperance leaders that culminated in a national convention of Catholic temperance societies in Baltimore in March 1872. The association that emerged consisted of local parish societies organized into state unions, each state union a part of the national. Each local union was required to have a spiritual director, preferably the parish pastor. The union proposed to be explicity Catholic and from the beginning was heavily influenced by the clergy. Its first President, the Rev. James McDevitt, a Washington, D. C. priest, had once been a heavy drinker. Elected first vice president by acclamation, O'Brien begged off but consented to act as treasurer.[40] Between 1872 and 1885 the national union grew until it included 634 local societies and almost forty thousand members.[41] We will concern ourselves here with the early years of the movement, examining its relationship with concepts of respectability and with Irish nationalism. The C. T. A. U. movement was very much a reaction to the way the Irish were perceived in the larger society.

From its beginning, the movement concerned itself

with the image of the drunken Irishman, an image that colored American thinking of things both Irish and Catholic. In issuing the call for the first national convention, O'Brien justified the union as able to disperse "a multitude of aspersions upon . . . [Catholic] religion," and show "to our fellow citizens of other denominations" that through "the inspiration of religion" Catholics, also, could practice temperance.[41] The <u>Irish American</u> thought that the Baltimore convention and ensuing national union "are doing more than has ever been effected, heretofore, to cast from the Irish name the unmerited stigma our enemies would fain attach to it."[42] A year later the <u>Irish World</u> expressed similar thoughts more directly. Noting that the union was primarily a temperance and religious society, the C. T. A. U. nevertheless "necessarily" promised to "help to accomplish many reforms, and [to] present a solid front to every assault made by bigotry and prejudice upon the Irish and Catholic element."[43] At a Fort Lee, New Jersey temperance rally, O'Brien claimed that as much liquor was consumed by the rich as by the poor, but the rich "have the means to hide their vice and the poor people have not." The poor, therefore, must take even more care to be temperate.[44] Drunkenness, Father Patrick Hennessy, the ardent spiritual director of the New Jersey union told a Jersey City audience, "is our bane and curse, and if we would preserve our standing here among the various races which dwell in this Republic, we need to exterminate that fell vice of intoxication from among us."[45]

Concern for what the native-born thought of the Irish expressed itself in other ways. When Bishop Bayley spoke at a monster temperance rally in Jersey City in November 1871, the *Irish American* devoted part of its coverage to "OPINION OF THE AMERICAN POPULATION." Quoting the *American Standard* and *Evening Journal*, "whose praise is ever sparingly given to anything emanating from Irishmen or Catholics," it noted the favorable reports in those two papers.[46] When the Rev. John Boylon of Crosserlaugh returned to Ireland from a visit to the United States, he wrote, "In the eyes of the American people nothing so much elevates an Irishman as strict teetotalism. It actually makes him a different man."[47]

While Americans might see temperate and non-temperate Irishmen as somewhat different, they were not, apparently, different enough. At the 1872 New Jersey state convention O'Brien urged the union to eschew politics, including cooperation with Protestant temperance societies. The proper sphere for Catholic temperance was the individual reformation of Catholics. "By entangling our associations in political operations," he said, "we would endanger our success in our proper sphere." Unstated but clearly implied in his remarks was a belief that Catholic attempts to influence even temperance legislation would be bitterly opposed by Protestants, even by Protestants with similar goals. As a student of Jersey City politics, O'Brien was well aware of the hysteria that aggressive Catholic attempts to influence legislation or policy could bring forth. Nor was he far wrong. In 1876 an <u>Evening Journal</u> correspondent lumped Catholic total abstinence societies in with other "treasonable secret organizations of the Papal Church" that sought to undermine American institutions.[48]

While the Catholic Total Abstinence Union played no role in American politics, it nevertheless attempted both to use and advance the Irish national cause. A placard at a Jersey City rally in late 1871 keynoted the theme: "Irish Sobriety means Irish Unity; thence Irish Liberty." When the Very Rev. Thomas N. Burke, O. P., a visiting Irish Dominican, spoke at an outdoor rally in Jersey City, he pressed the same theme:

> The man who is exiled for his love of country will aid that country to achieve her independence and her nationality, by the strength, the power, and the influence of his genius and of his virtue (loud cheers). I associate with this virtue of temperance, which I preach to you--I associate with that all my hopes not only for your individual domestic happiness,--all my hopes for your eternal salvation,--but I associ-

> ate with this virtue of temperance all my hopes
> of my native land,--for her future happiness--
> for her future glory (great enthusiasm).[49]

Again and again C. T. A. U. rhetoric stressed the need for sober Irishmen to defeat the British tyranny.

Concern for Ireland expressed itself more directly in an attempt to export the movement to Ireland itself. Representing the New Jersey union, John J. O'Mahony, Secretary of the New Jersey union and a business associate of O'Brien's, toured Ireland in early 1873 to investigate the feasibility of affiliated Irish total abstinence societies. Irish affiliates would have two purposes: to carry the cause to every Irish tippler, and to act as conduits for emigrants. Using a common membership card, those who left Ireland would be met and immediately entered on the rolls of an American society which would then work to orient the new member.[50] O'Mahony returned encouraged, predicting "an uprising of the people for temperance . . . all over our native land."[51] This program, however, was beyond the resources of the New Jersey union. At the next meeting of the national union's Board of Governors, O'Brien introduced a resolution to make exportation of the movement to Ireland national union policy. The resolution adopted, O'Mahony returned to Ireland late in 1873 on behalf of the national union. His visit did not, however, produce the expected results. For obscure reasons, the national union dropped this policy and left the business of contacting new arrivals to local societies.[52]

After 1873, the Catholic temperance societies fell on hard times. Economic depression decimated the ranks as members moved about in search of work. From 1875 to 1880, the C. T. A. U. suffered a gradual decrease in members, a condition not reversed until the return of prosperity. Additionally, the national union embarked on a fund-raising campaign to build a fountain in honor of the United States centennial. Erected in Philadelphia at a cost of $50,000, the fountain portrayed Moses surrounded by four prominent Catholics, Archbishop Carroll, Commodore Barry, Father Mathew, and Charles Carroll of Carrollton. Here were the status aspirations of Irish Catholics cast in marble and bronze.[53]

The C. T. A. U. played an important role in the 1870's and deserves further study for a variety of reasons. Not only did it partially fill the gap in Irish nationalist activity between the Fenians and the Land League (which it endorsed in 1881), but it drew large numbers of Irish together to meet the challenge of a hostile social environment. In Jersey City the central figure came out of the Young Democrats and was by no means a poor man. Neither were others prominent locally. Patrick McNulty, an alderman in 1870, was treasurer of the state union in 1873, and a large property owner. Patrick Meehan edited the important *Irish American*, and Charles H. O'Neill was mayor of Jersey City.

Who joined the Catholic total abstinence societies remains a question which needs detailed further study. The Irish community in Jersey City, as elsewhere in the 1870's, was primarily a working class community. While the C. T. A. U. leadership came largely from the Irish middle class, as a reform movement temperance cut across class lines. In *Drink and the Victorians* Brian Harrison has demonstrated that temperance appealed to many elements within the working class but especially to the working class elite.[54] The twenty Jersey City delegates to the New Jersey Catholic Total Abstinence Union convention in 1873 fit Harrison's thesis. Of the eleven who can be identified, only one was white collar, two--including James W. O'Brien--were proprictors, two laborers, and the other six skilled workers.[55] The Catholic total abstinence movement, furthermore, saw itself as complementing rather than opposing temperance, a concept that had broader working class appeal among Irish and non-Irish alike.[56] Detailed local research, especially in those areas where the C. T. A. U. was strongest, such as Philadelphia and New Jersey and Massachusetts towns and cities, will add to our knowledge of class interaction within the Irish community itself. That this interaction was complex is obvious. Middle class Young Democrats could not build a mass political base among the working class Irish in 1870, but the temperance movement that grew out of that attempt crossed class lines, using the rhetoric not only of temperance but also of Irish nationalism and traditional Catholicism. The experiences of the Young Democrats and the C. T. A. U. in Jersey City underscore the importance of understanding the inner dynamics of the Irish communities themselves before we can fully comprehend the relationship these communities had to the larger society in Gilded Age American cities.

DOCUMENTATION: CHAPTER VI

[1] <u>New York World</u>, March 28, 1861.

[2] Stephan Thernstrom, <u>Poverty and Progress: Social Mobility in a Nineteenth Century City</u> (Atheneum ed., New York, 1969), pp. 171-180. Thernstrom probably overstates the degree of Catholic integration into the community. While admitting the ambivalent attitude towards Catholicism on the part of the native-born, he still seems to equate the quest for Irish votes with the integration of Irish Catholics into the larger community.

[3] The election was tainted with charges of vote-buying and naturalization frauds. <u>New York Times</u>, October 28, November 8, 11, 28, 1868.

[4] <u>New York Herald</u>, September 3, 1870.

[5] <u>Ibid.</u>, September 10, 1870; <u>Jersey City Gazette</u>, September 10, 1870; <u>New York Sun</u>, October 29, 1870.

[6] <u>Jersey City Herald</u>, September 17, 1870.

[7] <u>Ibid.</u>, June 4, 1870.

[8] <u>Journal</u>, October 13, 1870.

[9] <u>Ibid.</u>

[10] <u>Ibid.</u>, November 1, 1870; <u>New York Herald</u>, September 12, 30, 1870; <u>Irish American</u>, October 6, 1869; <u>Jersey City Herald</u>, November 5, 1870.

[11] <u>Newark Daily Advertiser</u>, October 7, 1870.

[12] <u>Journal</u>, October 22, 1870.

[13] <u>Newark Daily Advertiser</u>, October 11, 1870.

[14] <u>Standard</u>, November 8, 1870. At a meeting of the Irish Emigrant Aid and Land Colonization Society, O'Bierne said, ". . . land is power, land is respectability, land is wealth, and say what you will, after all, the owners of the land are the pillars of the state." <u>Journal</u>, June 4, 1870.

[15] <u>Standard</u>, November 2, 1870.

[16] *Jersey City Herald*, November 5, 1870.

[17] *New York Herald*, October 3, 1870.

[18] *Journal*, November 1, 1870.

[19] Ibid.

[20] *Newark Daily Advertiser*, October 18, 1870.

[21] Ibid., October 29, 1870; *Jersey City Herald*, November 5, 1870.

[22] *Newark Daily Advertiser* and *Journal*, October, 1870, passim.

[23] *Journal*, November 5, 1870; *Standard*, November 9, 1870.

[24] *Jersey City Herald*, November 12, 1870; *Jersey City Times*, November 9, 1870.

[25] *Irish World*, November 2, 1870; *New York Herald*, November 2, 1870.

[26] *Standard*, November 9, 1870.

[27] *New York Sun*, October 29, 1870.

[28] See, for example, William V. Shannon, *The American Irish* (New York, 1963), pp. 60-67.

[29] *New York Freeman's Journal and Catholic Register*, May 30, 1874; *New York Herald*, November 2, 1870.

[30] See following chapter.

[31] Sister Joan Bland, *Hibernian Crusade: The Story of the Catholic Total Abstinence Union of America* (Lancaster, 1951), pp. 9-48.

[32] Ibid., p. 53.

[33] Manuscript census, Jersey City, 1860, Ward 4, pt. 2, p. 55; 1870, Ward 8, p. 26.

[34] *New York Sun*, April 8, 1868; *Journal*, April 10, 1868; *Standard*, April 11, 1868. Perhaps with hopes of political advancement, O'Brien kept a large advertisement for his New York stationers business in the *Standard* during these months.

[35] *Irish American*, August 15, 1868.

[36] *New York Herald*, October 7, 1870; *Journal*, November 8, 1870; *Manual . . . 1870-1871*, pp. 43-44.

[37] *Irish American*, February 4, 1871.

[38] *Ibid.*, July 8, 1871.

[39] *Irish World*, August 17, 1872.

[40] *Irish American*, March 2, 1872.

[41] James W. O'Brien, ed., *Catholic Temperance Textbook*, p. 51, quoted in Bland, p. 67.

[42] *Irish American*, January 27, 1872.

[43] *Irish World*, April 19, 1873.

[44] *Irish American*, March 23, 1872.

[45] *Irish World*, November 25, 1871.

[46] *Irish American*, December 9, 1871.

[47] *Irish World*, April 8, 1871.

[48] *Irish American*, February 10, 1872; *Journal*, April 10, 1876. The national union began to endorse political solutions to the liquor problem, such as high license, after 1880. Bland, pp. 94-95.

[49] *Irish American*, May 25, 1872; William John Fitzpatrick, *The Life of the Very Rev. Thomas N. Burke, O. P.* (London, 1894), p. 266.

[50] *Irish American*, May 31, 1873; *Irish World*, April 12, 1873.

[51] *Irish American*, May 31, 1873; for resolutions, see *Irish World*, May 31, 1873.

[52] *Irish American*, December 6, 1873; Joseph C. Gibbs, *History of the Catholic Total Abstinence Union of America* (Philadelphia, 1907), p. 30.

[53] The fountain apparently split the membership, with many, including O'Brien, opposing it. After 1876 he no longer accepted Union office. Gibbs, pp. 31-49; Bland, pp. 32-33.

[54] Brian H. Harrison, *Drink and the Victorians: The Temperance Question in England, 1815-1872* (Pittsburgh, 1971), pp. 19-36.

[55] *Irish World*, May 17, 1873.

[56] *Irish American*, February 10, 1872.

CHAPTER VII

NATIVISM AND THE 1871 COMMISSION CHARTER

The nature of the Board of Aldermen elected in April 1870 and the attempt by the Young Democrats to wrest political power from the old native-born leadership in November 1870 led directly to the end of local government in Jersey City. Threatened by the independence which the city's Irish had begun to show, native-born members of both parties closed ranks to restore the city government to native-born Protestant control. The events that followed the assembly election in 1870 revealed the depth of nativism that continued through the Civil War into the 1870's and the fear of Catholicism that men who had been Know-Nothings continued to feel.

The <u>Evening Journal</u>, the city's foremost exponent of anti-Catholicism, began agitating for a radical change in Jersey City's mode of government immediately after the November election. The 1870 charter of the consolidated city, which the <u>Journal</u> had approved the previous spring, now became an "ill-framed hodge-podge," investing too much power in too many aldermen. The <u>Journal</u> demanded a drastic cut in the number of aldermen and a divorce of such key public functions as public works, police, and fire protection from aldermanic control.[1] The <u>Journal</u> spoke for the native-born Protestant Republicans, men who considered themselves the natural elite and the moral leaders of the community. These men, uneasy in an immigrant city, wrote and instituted a charter that restored themselves to power, and then justified the result with arguments on the lack of fitness of lower class immigrants to govern an American city.

Created by the Jersey City Republican leadership, and enacted by the Republican legislature elected in November 1870, the charter replaced Democratic with Republican office-holders. The question of party, however, was less important than the moral posture and ethnic origins of the new government. Opposition from native-born Democrats was nominal and ineffectual. In fact, native-born Democrats used the opportunity of charter reform to excise an increasingly troublesome Irish majority from positions of influence within the party. The charter of 1871 must be understood in ethnic, not in mere party terms.

The Journal's agitation led to Republican meetings in all sixteen wards and the election of two delegates from each ward to attend a charter convention.[2] The convention convened on December 20, 1870, with the Journal's editor, Zebina K. Pangborn, in the chair. Although secrecy was intended, details quickly appeared in the press. Who should participate came up for discussion early in the session. While a few favored soliciting suggestions from the public, this idea "evoked considerable opposition" and was defeated. Mindful of their standing in the community, the delegates did not wish to appear "as if they hadn't brains enough to make a charter themselves." The convention then considered specific reforms. The owner of a large abattoir wanted a professional fire department. His firm, he claimed, paid over two hundred dollars annually above taxes for fire protection; under no circumstances, he felt, should fire or police protection be left to the Board of Aldermen. Frederick Goetze, a German restaurant owner, summed up convention hostility toward the sitting aldermen, by suggesting that they be left only the power to license saloons, impound strays, and run the public baths. "They want them," he said, "for their own unwashed."[3]

The convention met infrequently and with tighter secrecy after this initial meeting and assigned the preparation of a formal document to four men. These men shared a view of social order and political power characteristic of the middle class Republicans--the "respectability," as one paper called them--which demanded a revolution in city government. None of the four had been born in New Jersey, and all had ties to nativism, temperance, and anti-Catholicism. Zebina K. Pangborn edited the *Evening Journal*. He was born in rural Peacham, Vermont, where his father, a doctor, was an early abolitionist and teetotaler. After graduating from the University of Vermont, he taught school, edited an educational magazine, and then moved on, in the late 1850's, to edit the nativist *Boston Bee*. He served as a major in the Civil War, and then joined a brother in Jersey City, where he edited a paper that was Republican in politics and anti-Catholic in religion.[4] James Gopsill was born in New York City to English parents. An active Know-Nothing in the 1850's, he was elected mayor on a temperance platform in 1867. His excessive zeal cost him re-election in 1868. When the *Jersey City Argus* exposed a secret anti-Catholic organization in 1876, Pangborn and Gopsill both appeared prominently on the rolls.[5]

The other two men responsible for the charter were British by birth. Jonathan Dixon, Jr., a lawyer and the charter's actual author, was born in Liverpool but raised in New Brunswick, where the Hardenbergh family, itself active in nativist politics, sponsored his legal education. A Congregationalist, he vocally supported temperance and evangelical activity among the local Catholics.[6] The fourth man, William Bumsted, Jr., was cut from slightly different cloth. His father, a staunch Baptist, had emigrated in 1836 after refusing to pay church rates in his native Norfolk. In Jersey City he founded a contracting business, and his son later founded his own firm, specializing in sewers and street repairs. Bumsted neither smoked nor drank--not even coffee or tea--and contributed to church-related causes. But while he had mastered the "Thou shalt not's," he was a child of the Gilded Age in the "Thou shalt's." His relationship to the street improvements in Bergen, where he had been an alderman before consolidation, was suspect, and he viewed the charter as much as a means of advancing his own contracting business as a means of furthering moral reform.[7]

Made public in late January 1871, the charter these men designed invested power in men as much like themselves as possible. Knowing that the New Jersey legislators were rural, native-born and Protestant, they placed authority in three five-man commissions appointed by the legislature. The charter granted the commissions broad powers to effect change in their respective spheres of city administration. Only by granting sweeping authority to those in office, the charter authors reasoned, could the government act quickly for the good of the community. Action, not debate, they hoped, would characterize the future regime. In charge of water, sewers, and streets, the Board of Public Works could order work begun, tear down or move obstructing buildings, and assess property benefited. With the aldermen and mayor consenting, they could charge improvements that benefited the city as a whole against the general taxation. The legal rights of individuals to obstruct unwanted improvements were severely circumscribed. In short, the board was to construct a general plan of integrated city improvements and execute it, over-riding local objections to individual works. The police commission also received important powers. Not only did the charter enlarge the force from one hundred to one hundred and thirty men, but the police received increased powers of summary arrest. They became a more effective agency for social control. Similarly, by vesting the power to appoint election officials in the police board, election turbulence, especially in lower class Irish districts, could more easily be controlled. The fire commissioners had more limited functions. They were to form a department with a professional core supported by volunteers, regulate explosives, and order unsafe buildings torn down. To finance the proposed government, the charter called for a Board of Finance and Taxation, consisting of the president of the police commission, the mayor, and the president of the Board of Aldermen. Conceived of as a body to gather and disperse funds in a business-like manner, this board was also, by its control of the purse strings, to act as a check on the other boards.

The mayor and aldermen thus lost their traditional power, and little remained for them to do. The mayor became a figurehead, sitting on one board and exercising a weak veto over the aldermen. That body licensed saloons, "hawkers, peddlers, butchers . . . omnibus drivers and porters," supervised the removal of nuisances from the streets, regulated the speed of locomotives, and, of course, ran the public baths. When the charter was approved, the appointed boards would run the city, and the aldermen would clean up behind.[8]

To prevent the specter of lower class immigrants regulating the speed of locomotives in Jersey City, the charter proposed a redistricting of the city, replacing the sixteen wards with six aldermanic districts. The redistricting concentrated as many Irish as possible into one horseshoe-shaped district. This deliberate gerrymander, quickly dubbed "the horseshoe," encompassed the tenement districts along the Hudson River docks and Erie right-of-way and the swampland shanties at the base of Bergen Hill.[9]

Submitted to the public and the legislature simultaneously, the charter lacked only the names of the fifteen initial commissioners. These were to be supplied by the legislature. The *Evening Journal* printed the entire charter proposal during the last week in January and praised it editorially. The new charter was clear and explicit, decipherable "without the help of a lawyer." Firmly fixing responsibility for action at all levels of administration, it removed the city "out of the control of ward politicians, office seekers, and gin mill influences." Most importantly, Jersey City, whose consolidation was still more political than physical, needed a Board of Public Works with "a just, feasible, practical plan for public improvements," administered in a manner both "practical

MAP II
DISTRICT BOUNDARIES, JERSEY CITY, 1871

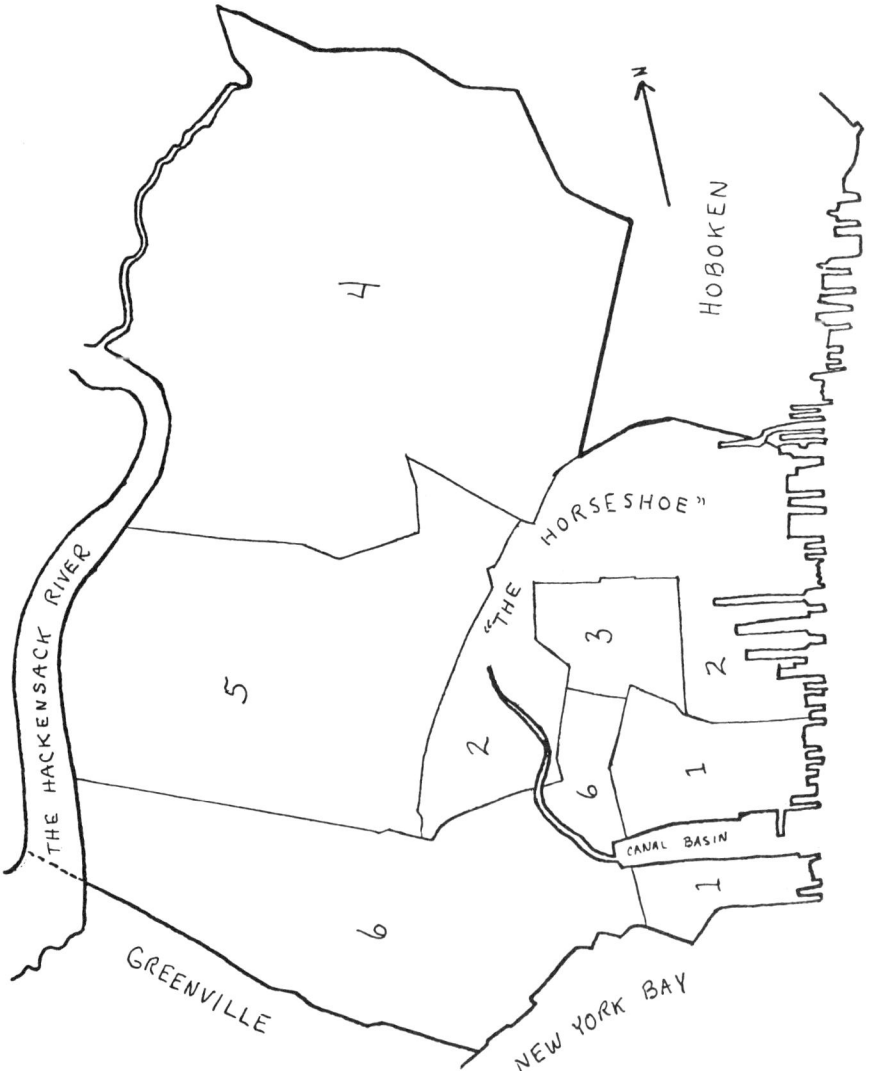

and efficient." And public improvements were "demanded by every business interest." The <u>Journal</u> felt that men elected from single wards could never adopt a "general system" of improvements because they would "necessarily represent their own particular localities to such a degree" that no one would represent the city as a whole. To be efficient, city management should be placed "in a small body of competent men," rather than in a heterogeneous body of thirty-two aldermen.[10]

The rhetoric of managerial efficiency in government is usually associated with the Progressive era, when government on business principles became a watchword of municipal reform. Samuel Hays has argued rather persuasively that the municipal reform movement of the early twentieth century was essentially an upper class movement to deprive lower class people of much of their representation in their city's affairs. Reform rhetoric concealed a view that the entire community's interests could best be served with businessmen as municipal decision-makers. They assumed that the institutionalization of their own values would advance the common good.[11] The Jersey City charter reform movement of 1871 had the same goals, but lacked even the pretense of democratic rhetoric.

The concept of business government masked as much as it revealed. Crucial to an understanding of municipal reform is an understanding that a "businessman" was almost by definition a native-born Protestant in 1910 as well as in 1870. Seventy percent of Jersey City's native-born aldermen in 1870 were of the economic elite, compared with only twenty percent of the immigrants. All of the native-born aldermen were Protestant; sixty percent of the immigrants were Catholic. To form a business government meant to form a native-born Protestant government, a factor too little appreciated in discussions of municipal reform. Nor were state-appointed commissions a new device to insure that control of a city remained with its native-born elite. The New York legislature, at the request of local reformers, created a police commission for New York City in 1857 in order "to have their standards of upper-middle-class morality enforced uniformly throughout the city . . . police reorganization was designed to that end."[12] Jersey City had a similar commission from 1866 to 1868, and at least a dozen other cities experimented with police commissions after the Civil War as a means of controlling their lower class immigrant citizens.[13] The use of non-elected commissions, then, was hardly new when in 1900 a Texas governor appointed three men to rebuild Galveston, sparking another round of "business" governments. The Gilded Age was in its infancy when "Progressivism" came to Jersey City.

The <u>American Standard</u> spoke for the native-born wing of the Democratic party. Edited by John Lyons, a former

Know-Nothing, it never opposed the basic form of governmental change. Native-born Democrats were on the defensive in 1871. Middle class Irishmen, under the leadership of Aeneas Fitzpatrick, sought, in the fall of 1870, to dislodge completely the party's native-born leadership. While electing none of their own candidates, the Young Democrats did scuttle the regular Democratic assembly slate and an incumbant Congressman, Orestes Cleveland, also a former Know-Nothing. This Irish push from within the Democratic party threatened native-born Democrats more than the Republican push from without. In reviewing the charter proposal, the <u>Standard</u> did not oppose the basic form of government, but only the details. The "unlimited power" given the Board of Public Works would "corrupt our good men." Setting the aldermen as a check on the Board's decisions would save the commissioners from themselves. The <u>Standard</u> never suggested that the commissioners would be other than "our good men."[14]

The weekly <u>Jersey City Herald</u> differed sharply. Owned and edited by Hugh McDermott, who identified with Irish nationalism and the city's poor, it condemned the charter roundly as an attempt by a small part of the citizenry to grab the entire city. This was the "Thieves Charter," investing power in the "Board that Works the Public," which would "control everything" in the city. McDermott saw no difference between the opportunity to abuse power and the abuse itself.[15]

The problem of erecting a system that allowed the broad exercise of power while protecting against corruption disturbed Republicans as well as Democrats. Leading Republicans met on January 30 to review the recently unveiled charter. Dixon, the document's author, was hard-pressed to defend the powers granted the Board of Public Works. His chief antagonist, lawyer Jacob Weart, was also an expert in municipal government, and as strong a supporter of Protestant causes as Dixon himself. Weart saw the charter as open-ended, as inviting abuse, and demanded at least a limit on total annual expenditures. Dixon brushed the argument aside. "The only safeguard necessary," he said, "was to place honest, energetic men in the Board, for no legislation can be framed to prevent a dishonest man from being corrupt." Dixon placed his faith in the right men, Weart in the right measures.[16]

But who were the "right" men? By Dixon's own definition of the charter, its rise or fall depended on whom the legislature named as commissioners. Alderman William H. Thomas, a Methodist Sunday School superintendent, "was willing to give the compilers of the charter all due credit," but was also "happy to know that some of them would not have a hand in carrying out its provisions."[17] A moral government demanded moral men, or at least men with a shared definition of morality. The charter supporters, however, differed over how the powers granted the Board of Public Works should be used. Were they to be a sacred trust or a golden opportunity? Many contractors viewed the great power as a prelude to great activity and great profits. The city would be improved whether it needed it or not. The key man here was Bumsted, a contractor and one of the charter's authors. While he served as an alderman in Bergen and as chairman of the improvements committee, the city was "improved" to the brink of bankruptcy, and Bumsted had been censured by the courts for voting on contracts in which he had an interest. Dixon had not designed the charter with men like this in mind, but Bumsted eagerly sought a seat on the Board of Public Works, and received vocal support from those who hoped to profit from contracts.[18]

This meeting of Republicans, therefore, chose from among themselves a prudential committee to lobby for the charter in the state legislature, and at the same time, keep the city from falling into the hands of "a few unscrupulous men." A few days later they journeyed to Trenton to meet with the Hudson County Republican legislators. If they approved the charter, the Republican party, in control of both houses, would routinely pass it as a local measure. They found the four Assemblymen receptive to the charter but adamant on including Bumsted on the Board of Public Works. This impasse brought the charter's progress to an abrupt halt.[19]

A week later the prudential committee reported back to the city's Republicans. Benjamin F. Welsh, a real estate agent and a member of the committee, reviewed the week's events and the impasse over appointments. William J. Stitt, a New York merchant, then moved that the meeting show faith in its prudential committee. The large number of contractors who had attended to support Bumsted shouted this down, and someone introduced a second resolution demanding that the meeting show faith in the Assembly delegation. An equally loud, although perhaps more dignified uproar came from Bumsted's opponents. The chairman, Dudley S. Gregory, called for order, then threatened to leave. A speedy adjournment followed, by self-conscious gentlemen, "anxious that a Republican meeting should not be disgraced by the rowdy element which had been injected into it."[20]

The charter lay dormant for another month as various groups lobbied for it and against it. Eventually the prudential committee and the assemblymen worked out a compromise that enlarged the Board of Public Works to seven members, among them Bumsted, and reduced that Board's influence on the Board of Finance. By the beginning of March the charter was ready for the legislative journey.[21]

Effective opposition never crystalized in Jersey City. The Bumsted question split the Republican party on policy, but not on philosophy. After the noisy Republican meeting of February 6, the <u>Jersey City Times</u>, a Republican paper, called for the defeat of the charter as "fatally defective," not because it ended local government, but because it gave unrestricted power without effective checks. The <u>Times</u> continued to favor a centralized government, but only if "honesty" could somehow be built into the structure.[22]

The Board of Aldermen attempted to organize itself into a focus of opposition, but failed. On February 7, Alderman Patrick Sheeran, a blunt Irish carriage maker, denounced Pangborn, Dixon, and Bumsted and moved that the aldermen travel to Trenton in a body to lobby against the charter. Alderman Thomas, who at a Republican meeting had given the charter's compilers "all due credit," now hoped "that his party would not father it." He opposed the aldermanic junket to Trenton, however, because the aldermen were so "notoriously corrupt" that they "would not be courteously received." Sheeran's measure failed, and the aldermen finally passed a weak resolution which requested Mayor Charles H. O'Neill to call a public meeting. Held three days later, the meeting was poorly attended and contented itself with passing resolutions repudiating "all and every act of our Assembly representatives which tends to deprive the People of the right to elect their own Executors under the laws."[23]

The German population watched the charter proceedings with interest and trepidation. Before the charter was officially public, on January 12, the German Central Organization denounced appointed commissions as "entirely repugnant to the principles of self-government," and "in collision with republican institutions." But these doubts aside, by February leading Germans sought to protect their interests in the city by seating their countrymen on the commissions. The German Central Organization met on February 7 and nominated a member for each commission, on the theory that as they constituted twenty percent of the Republican strength, they deserved one fifth of the commission seats. The nominees were successful small businessmen, active in the organizational affairs of the German community. The meeting then appointed a committee of three to lobby in Trenton, and this committee succeeded in gaining a German seat on the Police and Public Works Boards.[24]

Irish opposition remained ineffectual and fragmented. Without legislative representation, and with no leverage within the Republican party, they were cut off from all consideration. The charter did not come as a surprise to the city's Irish, however, and they were well aware that it was directed against them. During the closely fought legislative campaign of November 1870, an open letter, purportedly from a number of local Fenians, urged support for the regular Democrats over the Fitzpatrick ticket. A

Democratic split, they claimed, would ensure a Republican legislative delegation which would then "commission the Police, Water and other Public Departments of the city, laying out hundreds of Irishmen now in their employ, and Irishmen won't handle a policeman's club, nor any other official badge for ten years."[25] When the Republicans did attempt to commission the government, the Fitzpatrick Democrats, representing Irish "respectability," abandoned their poorer countrymen and attempted to gain recognition from the charter convention and a seat on one of the commissions. John A. Donnelly, a restaurant owner, attended the Republican meeting of February 5 and urged an alliance with the Fitzpatrick forces, but was soundly rebuffed. The origin of the charter was too deeply steeped in nativism and anti-Catholicism to allow a compromise with the Irish, regardless of their claim to respectability. "James Gopsill," claimed Frederick W. Wolbert, a Catholic auctioneer, "has said that no Irishman shall go upon that commission." Although indignation meetings took place in several heavily Irish wards during February, they received only the briefest notice in the press.[26]

Native-born Democrats played an enigmatic role. With few exceptions they held their tongues and allowed their party to be deposed from local power without active opposition. An anonymous correspondent to the *Jersey City Times* claimed that John Lyons and Orestes Cleveland were as responsible for the charter as Bumsted, Gopsill, and Pangborn. Given the fact that Lyons and Cleveland were both former Know-Nothings and had led the native-born wing of the Democratic party since 1860, this was perfectly plausible. Pangborn and Gopsill also had been Know-Nothings. That they had reached some sort of agreement was indicated by the charter itself, which specified two official papers for the city, Pangborn's Republican-nativist Evening Journal, and Lyons's Democratic-nativist American Standard. The Standard opposed the charter weakly and unconvincingly, and berated the Jersey City Herald for associating the charter with thievery and plunder before the commissioners were actually named.[27]

Although the issue of excluding Irishmen seldom entered the public controversy over the charter directly, it lurked beneath the surface of all public discussion. When the Evening Journal talked of "capable and efficient government," its readers knew that editor Pangborn had attacked Irish office-holders for four years, had charted the growth of Irish influence with alarm, and had once suggested a six-month aldermanic recess, "so the oneddicated part of the kouncil kud hev the advantage of the Primary Skool."[28] There was no real need to approach this issue directly; it was too well understood. It was also unwise to exacerbate ethnic tensions unnecessarily when native-born Protestants were a distinct minority. There were many nativists in Jersey City in 1871, but no self-proclaimed Know-Nothings. Commission government was advanced in the name of efficiency, but is best understood in terms of class, ethnicity, and religion. The purpose of the charter was to restore native-born Protestants to office, and purge the city of lower class Irish and Catholic influence. Republicans carried out the task and would fill the appointed offices as they controlled the state legislature. Influential Democrats played their part by staying out of the way.

The charter began to work its way through the legislature in early March, meeting unexpected opposition from Republicans who saw the measure as unwise and detrimental to state-wide Republican interests. The charter, some Republicans feared, would prove unpopular and alienate voters in all parts of the state. The Republican Newark Daily Advertiser editorialized in this vein.

> . . . the bill is recalcitrant. It will kick back without mercy. It will withdraw the Republican party of our sister city from all popular sympathy and fair and honorable power of appeal. No matter who are made commissioners in matters of police and taxation, there comes a time when the minor attains his majority and insists upon being his own master. He leaves father and mother and cleaves to his own and the most paternal government in the world is an insult to his self-respect and common sense. Every man hates an agent forced upon him by a legislative guardianship.
>
> It is the decency of Jersey City that calls for commissions, and we are very sure that the decency

> will find that it has made a frightful mistake.
> To draw near and keep close to the common people
> is the wiser political strategy for the Republican
> party.

"Two prominent Republican Senators," reported the <u>New York Herald</u>, would oppose the bill, "because it would entail inevitable defeat on their party."[29]

Debate was <u>pro forma</u> in both houses of the legislature. The decision to pass had been made before and outside of the legislative process. Debate in the Assembly centered on an amendment to the charter to provide for popular ratification. Introduced by Michael Coogan, the only Democratic representative from Jersey City, it called for implementation only after approval by the city's voters. After it was rejected on a party-line vote, Austin H. Paterson of Monmouth suggested that a vote of only twenty-five percent be required for approval. This was similarly rejected. Paterson then claimed that the charter "was legislation not for the people but against the people. It was legislation for a few contractors, and no remedy was left to the people but to bend their necks to the yoke." His arguments did not prevail. The charter passed the Senate on March 20, 1871, again on appeals to party loyalty rather than on its merits. Only lawyer Leon Abbett, who opposed the movement from the start, and Police Chief Nathan Fowler, who would lose his job if it passed, worked with Hudson's Democratic Senator, Noah

Taylor, to defeat the bill. It then went to the Governor.[30]

Governor Theodore F. Randolph vetoed the charter, writing a veto message that showed both his sympathies with the charter authors and his objections to the charter as written. Randolph came from an old New Jersey family, and had made his money as a Jersey City lawyer and as president of the Morris and Essex Railroad. A Know-Nothing from 1852 until 1860, he was sent to the legislature in the latter year by a coalition of Jersey City Democrats and Know-Nothings. The same coalition elevated him to the governorship in 1868, and to the United States Senate in 1871. A Jersey City Irishman told an Irish World reporter in 1871, "Scratch Governor Randolph until he bleeds, and you will be sure to come upon a Know-Nothing in the full regalia of the order."[31]

In his veto message, Randolph found the charter to be "anti-republican in form--arbitrary in spirit and purpose, it can only be defended, if defensible at all, upon the ground that within the limits of Jersey City, at least, the principles of our forms of government--Federal, State and Municipal--are supposed to be valueless." This, however, he would readily admit:

> It may be true that local representative government, as carried on in our big cities, is found to work unfortunately. I am prepared to believe almost any

representation made to me upon this head. So long, however, as we profess to believe that the true policy of our government is to extend the privilege of the ballot to all men, regardless of their intelligence, interests, or other qualifications, just so long will we be faced by the dangers which legislation like that I object to seeks to obviate.

The problems in Jersey City, the desire for commissions which would "take away from the people . . . all the essentials of power in local government," stemmed from "the evils of an ill-regulated suffrage." Randolph did not oppose vesting power in the type of men that the charter's framers had in mind; he objected only to the manner. Perhaps with New York City's unhappy experiences with commissions in mind, he continued, "Legislative commissions, however constituted for good, are only pretended panaceas, at best; and at worst they will cure the ills by destroying the body." But with a restricted franchise, "the industrious, well meaning and thrifty citizens of large cities" would be able to "nominate and elect honest, equitable and intelligent representatives to their local boards and State Legislature." The respectability of a city belonged at its head, Randolph believed, and to ensure this, the franchise should be reserved for those who knew their social duty.

A dozen specific objections to charter provisions followed this discursive preamble. These dealt largely with details of finance and taxation which Randolph found in conflict with the state constitution. The heart of the veto was its preamble, and here Randolph showed not only his sympathy with the basic nativist sentiments of his former political allies, the authors of the charter, but also his fear of centralized government, remote from the people, a distinguishing characteristic of conservative Democrats in the Civil War era.[32]

The veto returned the charter to the legislature. A bitter fight then erupted in the Republican caucus as to the wisdom of over-riding the veto. One Assemblyman called the charter "a disgrace to the party" which would lead to "merited condemnation and defeat." But the Jersey City representatives, backed by the Jersey City charter supporters, remained adamant. At the third caucus meeting on the subject, the vote to over-ride was made a party measure, assuring the necessary votes to enact the charter.[33]

The charter became law on March 29, 1871, and took effect immediately. The seventeen commissioners named in the document were sworn into office and began the job of organizing a new government. The seven members of the Board of Public Works organized on April 2. They were all Protestants and all substantial businessmen. In general, their financial interests were of more than local scope. Two were in the cattle business, buying livestock in the west for slaughter in Jersey City and sale in the New

York market. Another was a retired New York agent for the Norwich and Worcester Railroad, and a fourth dealt in wholesale groceries in New York. Benjamin F. Welsh, prominent on the prudential committee that lobbied for the charter, owned much real estate in and around Jersey City. Only two had interests strictly on a local scale, and both were immigrants. The controversial Bumsted dealt in street and sewer improvements, and August Ingwerson, from Holstein, ran a successful ornamental painting business. Divorced from ward and neighborhood ties, they were the type of men that the Journal felt could adopt a "general system" of city improvements.[34] They were also the type of men that Samuel Hays found active in the Des Moines municipal reform movement of 1906, and the Pittsburgh movement of 1911.[35]

The commission's first business was to elect a president. Morrille H. Gillette, who operated a large slaughterhouse, defeated Bumsted by a vote of four to three, and many local Republicans breathed easier. By the same vote, the board defeated Bumsted's nominees for chief engineer and clerk, and they chose Jonathan Dixon, Jr., the charter's author, as their counsel. Bumsted's defeat was not without repercussions. Although the legislature would shortly adjourn, Z. K. Pangborn and other Republicans petitioned the legislature to amend the charter by adding two Democrats to the board, making it "bi-partisan," and

invalidating the previous vote for president. The two
hand-picked Democrats would then give Bumsted a five-to-
four majority. While unsuccessful, this maneuver further
illustrates the cultural, as distinct from the party,
roots of the charter.[36]

The Board of Police Commissioners organized the following night, with Ezekiel Pritchard, a businessman, the unanimous choice for President. These five men had backgrounds similar to those of the public works commissioners; additionally, *all* were temperance men, and they celebrated their organization with bowls of chowder. Four were native-born, and Frederick A. Goetze, the man who offered the aldermen the care of the public baths, was German.[37] When Salmon W. Hoyt, President of the old elected police board, turned over the records to the new board, he asked them to be fair in making removals, that one hundred and ten of the one hundred and thirty officers and men were competent and honest. But the new board had not been chosen to continue Irishmen in office. Commissioner Goetze told a *New York Sun* reporter that he would vote for Americans first, and Germans second. "But Irishmen, he says, are nowhere."[38]

In early May the *Irish World* reviewed the Police Commission's proceedings under the headline, "The Guillotine at Work--No Irish Need Apply." Men who had survived previous changes in administration were dismissed because "the fiat had gone forth that the Irishmen on the force, or a majority of them, were doomed." When a petition for appointment signed by Aeneas Fitzpatrick and James Brann, both prominent Irishmen, came before the commission, Commissioner Edmundson "remarked snappishly, 'I wonder they do not ask for all the appointments.'" The <u>Journal</u> objected to one Irish appointee, but the <u>Times</u> responded that the officer was Protestant Irish, and therefore acceptable.[39]

Other considerations governed the choice of a chief. The two candidates were Edward L. McWilliams, a Jersey City native who had been on the force from 1866 to 1868, and then worked as a special policeman for the Erie Railroad, and Benjamin Van Riper, a reprobate turned temperance lecturer and a local Republican organizer of some repute.[40] Choosing professionalism over zeal by appointing McWilliams, the commissioners soon received a petition signed by sixty prominent Republicans favoring Van Riper, and a bitter card appeared in the local press from the disappointed candidate, who blamed his defeat on liquor influence inside the citadel:

> And now let me say that one of the charges brought against me is that I am a "Temperance Man." Well, that is so. I had no idea that it was a crime to be one, and if it is, my only regret is that I had not been one ten years ago; but if I had it in my power, and drinking one drop of liquor would make me Chief of Police or Mayor of

> this City, I would refuse. No office in the gift of the people will ever prompt me, as long as I live, to buy or drink a drop of liquor.

His police career doused with cold water, Van Riper accepted a patronage job at the customs house two weeks later. That the card appeared at all is indicative of what many native-born citizens expected from their new government.[41]

Although specific attacks on Catholicism formed no part of the rhetoric of charter reform, events five years later revealed the depth of anti-Catholic feeling among those who wrote and instituted the charter of 1871. The Jersey City Argus, edited by Michael Malone, a second-generation Irish Catholic, began publication in 1875. In April 1876 he published an expose of the Order of the American Union, a secret society dedicated to preventing public aid to Catholic schools and charities. The Argus published the names of almost four hundred Jersey City members, and among them were seven of the seventeen commissioners, the entire staff of the Evening Journal, and many others who supported the charter.[42] The order probably began in Jersey City in 1874, and in no way originated or fostered the charter. The point is that a large number of those who created and instituted a "capable and efficient" government for Jersey City in 1871 participated in an explicitly anti-Catholic secret society five years later. Anti-Catholic and anti-Irish prejudices mingled freely and could not be separated. No one better expressed the confusing amalgam of class, religious and ethnic feelings that produced the 1871 charter than O. A. U. member Henry Callo, a barely literate insurance agent, who tried to explain the order in a letter to the <u>Argus</u>:

> My private opinion is that many of the members of the O. A. U. confound Catholicism with Irishism, consequently any act of an Irishman which effects public policy is attributed to the Romish Church. This confusing of things lead many to blame the Romish Church for acts for which she is not answerable.
> The love of country is so inborn in the constitution of an Irishman that in many case unfits him to be placed in positions of trust in a free republican form of government. He is disposed often to be turbulent. His desire to establish the independency of Ireland make him to be looked upon with a suspicious eye.
> This trait of character croping out warns the American people against putting to much confidence in him.[43]

The annual aldermanic election came only two weeks after the charter went into effect. Events at this election dramatically illustrated the "suspicious eye" through which native-born Protestants viewed the Irish. The new charter gerrymandered the city to dilute the Irish vote as much as possible. Native-born Democrats responded to the gerrymander by driving the Irish out of positions of power within the party, and allowing only native-born Democrats on the ballot. When the Democratic primary convention met on Saturday, April 8, Irishmen were excluded from party councils and completely left off the ballot. At the same time, the party abandoned "the horseshoe" to itself. When the *American Standard* printed the slate on April 10, it omitted the horseshoe nominations on the ground that such confusion prevailed that the regular Democratic candidates could not be ascertained. The ten candidates on the regular slate for the rest of the city were a study in nativism: five had been Know-Nothings in the 1850's and a sixth became an O. A. U. member later in the 1870's.[44]

The *American Standard* printed not one word on this silent *coup*, but the *Evening Journal* commented with approval:

> THE DEMOCRATIC NOMINATIONS
> THE THREAT EXECUTED
> THE KNOW-NOTHING COUNCILS PREVAIL
> NO IRISHMEN ON THE TICKET
> "ERIN GO BRAGH" TO TAKE A BACK SEAT
>
> Most of the Democratic candidates are from the old Know-Nothing wing who managed for so long to monopolize all the offices, while their Irish brethren did nearly all the voting. This course was resolved upon by some of the Democratic leaders, and was carried out in making nominations. It is serving a notice on the Irish voters to take a back seat-- telling them that they are good enough, as of old, to do the voting, but not the sort to put on the lead or be put into office. We knew they would get this back-handed slap someday, but they must settle the hash themselves.[45]

The Republican *Jersey City Times* felt that the Democrats had nominated "some of the best men in the city," and felt that this represented conscious imitation of the Republican "moral idea" concept which "exercises such a wholesome influence over its opponent."[46]

All ten of the regular Democratic nominees went down to defeat in the aldermanic election on April 11. An attempt to run an Irish slate in one district collapsed before election day, and Irishmen stayed home or voted Republican. The *New York Times* reported that "the Irishmen claim that they have the secret, and the neglect of the Irish element in the make up of the Democratic tickets--which bore no Irish names--did the business for the party." The *Jersey City Times* amplified on this theme: "There is a lack of confidence between the leaders and the led. The Irishmen who form the vast majority of the party have become tired of being used as a machine for the advancement of the selfish ends of a few corrupt politicians from the American wing of the party."[47]

Ten Republicans assumed seats on the reconstituted Board of Aldermen. Like their counterparts on the appointed boards, they were affluent and Protestant. One had been a Know-Nothing, and two later joined the O. A. U. Four were foreign-born, three British and one German. Two Irishmen sat on the board, elected from the "horseshoe" and recognized by neither party. Symbolic, perhaps, of both their backgrounds and their purpose, this body of aldermen broke with tradition and refused to review the St. Patrick's Day parade the following March.[48]

In the spring of 1871 the Irish of Jersey City were disenfranchised in three distinct ways. First the important functions of government were transferred to commissions appointed by the legislature. Second, the city was gerrymandered to dilute the Irish vote for what elected offices remained. Third, the native-born Democrats boldly threw the Irish out of the party hierarchy, although the Democratic ticket depended on Irish support for success.

The major theme of the spring of 1871 was ethnic and religious tension after the native-born Protestants found themselves displaced by Irish Catholics in municipal offices. Within the Democratic party itself, the native-born elite was rapidly losing control of an increasingly vocal and independent Irish electorate, who had scuttled a Congressman in 1870 and threatened worse for the future. Native-born Republicans and Democrats saw their conception of an ordered community about to smash against the values of men whom they saw as not a bit like themselves and a threat to society as they knew it. They fought the approaching defeat by changing the rules of the political game. Governor Randolph thought commissions indefensible unless, "within the limits of Jersey City, at least, the principles of all our forms of government--Federal, State, and Municipal--are supposed to be valueless." And that was exactly the point. To the men who framed the charter, a "moral idea" had been lost in Jersey City. The editor of the <u>Jersey City Times</u> considered the Democratic Know-

Nothing ticket of 1871 to contain "some of the best men in the city," and in the same editorial attempted to justify rule by an elite whether popularly supported or not:

> Society must always fail if it would make people truly honest; all it can do is restrict roguery by the application of wholesome discipline to every known manifestation thereof. It is, therefore, evident that an absolute necessity to the proper conservation of society is the continued success of the "Party of Great Moral Ideas."[49]

The editor, of course, meant the Republican party. But in Jersey City, in 1871, this conception of "honesty" and "wholesome discipline" was shared by those of a common Protestant and native-born heritage regardless of party. Democrats had opposed the additional powers the national government assumed to fight the Civil War, and in general opposed the extension of this philosophy of centralization to local government after the war. But the threat to a wider range of values posed by a government controlled by lower class Irish Catholics placed these Democrats in a very uncomfortable position: should they give up their control of city offices to immigrants who called themselves Democrats or to Republicans whose "great moral ideas" they but partially shared? That they chose to allow a wholly Republican government to assume control of the city, and then cast the Irish from the Democratic party itself, is an indication of the level of frustration and fear that native-born Americans felt in what John

Higham has chosen to call "The Age of Confidence."[50]

DOCUMENTATION: CHAPTER VII

¹*Journal*, March 30, November 25, 1870.

²*Ibid.*, December 13, 1870.

³*Jersey City Times*, December 20, 1870.

⁴Shaw, Vol. II, pp. 1119-1120; Ernest L. Bogart, Peacham, *The Story of a Vermont Hill Town* (Montpelier, 1948), p. 234.

⁵Shaw, Vol. II, pp. 1145-1146; *Jersey City Argus*, April 8, 1876.

⁶Shaw, Vol. II, pp. 1074-1075; McLean, p. 203.

⁷*Jersey City Herald*, August 13, 1870; September 12, 1874; *New York Tribune*, September 9, 1874.

⁸The *Jersey City Times* printed the entire charter proposal, January 25, 1871.

⁹*Charter of Jersey City and Supplements* (Jersey City, 1873), pp. 11-14. For maps, see *Standard*, April 5, 1871.

¹⁰*Journal*, January 30, February 1, 1871.

¹¹Samuel P. Hays, "The Politics of Reform in Municipal Government in the Progressive Era," *Pacific Northwest Quarterly*, Vol. 55, No. 4 (October, 1964), pp. 157-169.

¹²Richardson, pp. 81-86, 99. See also Roger Lane, *Policing the City: Boston, 1822-1885* (Cambridge, 1967), pp. 121-128.

¹³For a partial list of cities, see Richardson, p. 123.

¹⁴*Standard*, January 30, 1871.

¹⁵*Jersey City Herald*, January 28, February 11, 1871; *New York Tribune*, June 5, 1890.

¹⁶*Journal*, January 31, 1871.

¹⁷*Ibid.*

¹⁸*Jersey City Herald*, February through April, 1871, *passim*.

[19] Sackett, Vol. I, p. 87; *Jersey City Times*, January 31, February 1, 1871; *Journal*, February 2, 1871.

[20] *Journal* and *Jersey City Times*, February 6, 1871.

[21] *Journal*, February, 1871, *passim*.

[22] *Jersey City Times*, February 7, 1871.

[23] *Journal*, February 8, 1871; *Standard*, February 11, 1871. The *Journal* (February 11, 1871) called the meeting "a grand fizzle."

[24] *Standard*, February 2, 7; March 7, 1871; *Journal*, February 7, 1871.

[25] *Standard*, November 2, 1870.

[26] *Journal*, February 6, 1871; *Jersey City Times*, February 11, 1871; *Standard*, February 4, 1871.

[27] Letter to *Jersey City Times* (n.d.), reprinted in *Jersey City Herald*, March 4, 1871; *Standard*, February 22, 1871.

[28] *Journal*, October 21, 1868.

[29] *Newark Daily Advertiser*, March 25, 1871; *New York Herald*, March 10, 1871.

[30] *New York Herald*, March 1 and 10, 1871; *Journal*, March 18 and 24, 1871.

[31] Sackett, Vol. I, p. 109; Charles Robson, ed., *The Biographical Encyclopedia of New Jersey of the Nineteenth Century* (Philadelphia, 1877), pp. 557-558; *Irish World* (New York), August 12, 1871.

[32] Entire veto printed in *Newark Daily Advertiser*, March 25, 1871.

[33] *New York Herald*, March 25, 28 and 30, 1871.

[34] Short sketches of the public works commissioners appeared in the *Jersey City Times*, April 4, 1871.

[35] Hays, pp. 159-161.

[36] *Jersey City Times*, April 3, 6 and 7, 1871.

[37] Biographical information taken from city directories and census tracts.

[38] Jersey City Times, April 4, 1871; New York Sun, April 3, 1871.

[39] Irish World, May 6, 1871; Jersey City Times, April 22, 1871.

[40] For McWilliams, Journal, April 14, 1871. For Van Riper, Standard, December 30, 1870; Jersey City Times, April 12, 1871.

[41] Jersey City Times, April 14, 1871.

[42] The Jersey City Argus printed its expose between April 5 and April 8, 1876. National officers from Jersey City included Zebina K. Pangborn, editor of the Evening Journal, and George P. Edgar, a member of the charter convention in 1871. Edgar, claimed the New York Herald (December 21, 1875), initiated President Grant into the order in the summer of 1875.

[43] Jersey City Argus, April 10, 1876. Benjamin Van Riper, the defeated police chief aspirant of 1871, wrote, "I am proud to be a member, and what is more, I endorse its principles. I see no difference between a 'Know Nothing' of olden times and this new organization, except this is more liberal--admitting adopted citizens--'who are opposed to the destruction of our public schools.'" Journal, April 7, 1876.

[44] Standard, April 10, 1871.

[45] Journal, April 10, 1871.

[46] Jersey City Times, April 10, 1871.

[47] New York Times, April 12, 1871; Jersey City Times, April 11, 1871.

[48] Jersey City Times, April 12, 1871; New York Herald, March 18, 1873.

[49] Jersey City Times, April 10, 1871.

[50] John Higham, Strangers in the Land: Patterns of American Nativism, 1860-1925 (New York, Atheneum edition, 1970), pp. 12-34.

CHAPTER VIII

TRIALS AND ERRORS

1871 - 1877

> With fingers dirty and light,
> With eyes constantly crossed,
> A Commissioner sat in his own armchair,
> Counting of jobs the cost.
> "Steal! Steal! Steal!
> At every chance I get!
> Heed not the poor man's last appeal--
> There's room for more jobbing yet!"[1]

Commission government failed in Jersey City. Embarking on an ambitious program of improvements, the Board of Public Works not only increased the city debt but lost what little popular support it had. The commissions had a number of difficult jobs. To unify the three cities physically, the Board of Public Works had to build roads across the salt marsh and up the steep hill that separated lower Jersey City from Hudson and Bergen. Sewers had to be extended and relaid, always a problem in a city built largely on reclaimed land just above the water line. Many such projects met with resistance from local residents who did not see their need and resented the assessment. Pavonia Avenue was a case in point. Beginning at the Erie ferry, it ran north about six blocks to Hamilton Square, a small park, and stopped, to start again on the other side. Another segment ran from the park to the bottom of Bergen Hill, really a cliff at that point, and a third continued on top. The commissioners proposed connecting all segments by laying out a road from the Hudson to the Hackensack. Valuing their park, local residents objected vigorously and eventually killed the project, but not without much rancor and ill will.[2] This type of incident made the commissions seem that much more a remote autocracy, imposed on the city from without.

Further, public confidence in the commissioners rapidly evaporated. The Herald's doggerel caricature of the light-fingered, cross-eyed, heartlessly grasping commissioners gained increasing acceptance. The commissioners were corrupt. Common sense, if not concrete evidence, demanded that conclusion. The power granted the commissioners was so great and so remote from traditional popular checks that its abuse hardly required verification. Resentment and suspicion complemented each other in the public mind, especially as both the tax rate and public debt rose alarmingly.[3] Not surprisingly, Democrats campaigned against "that d----d charter" in the fall 1871 legislative elections. Leon Abbett assailed Jonathan Dixon, Jr., at rally after rally and made disfranchisement of the populace the major issue in the campaign.[4] Despite the 1871 gerrymander, Democrats elected four local assemblymen, the county's state senator, and the sheriff, besides providing a good majority for Joel Parker, the Democratic gubernatorial candidate. The charter, claimed the _Irish World_, had healed the wounds in the Democratic party. But the list of Democratic candidates in November 1871 made clear that the Irish had accepted, at least temporarily, a subordinate role in party affairs.[5]

When the _Jersey City Times_ reviewed the fall 1871 election, it also blamed the charter for Republican defeats. Mistrustful of the power given the appointed officials, voters had given credence to any rumors of abuse.[6] The _Times_ editor felt that the changes he had suggested the previous spring (giving the aldermen rather than the Board of Finance and Taxation final taxing and borrowing authority) would have prevented this loss of faith. More direct, the _Irish American_ claimed that the Republicans had "disgusted all thinking men, and created apathy and division among their former supporters."[7] Rapport between government and governed continued to deteriorate. In January 1872 the _Jersey City Times_ revealingly headlined an article about resistance to new improvements:

> BOARD OF WORKS
> OUR GOOD PROTESTANTS
> LESS FAITH AND MORE WORKS

The police commissioners also failed to live up to the promises of the previous spring. Speaking at a meeting of the City Mission and Tract Society in December 1871, Dixon himself criticized the police commissioners for failing to enforce "the laws in relation to the Sabbath rum traffic" on the specious grounds that "public sentiment was averse to it."[8]

As the zeal of the commissions' supporters diminished, the determination of their opponents increased. Resistance was overt by early 1872. Using the grand jury and the courts, the reunified Democrats put Bumsted in jail, deprived all five police commissioners of their citizenship, and frightened one fire commissioner out of town. The indictments and trials were more a response to the system of government than to the men who ran it, a fact acknowledged by all sides.

Newly elected Sheriff Rhinehart, born in Le Havre, France, empaneled a grand jury in January 1872. Supreme Court Judge Joseph D. Bedle urged them to root out official corruption. "There seems to be a spirit abroad," he lectured, "which winks at, if it does not actually encourage official dishonesty."[9] This charge was not unique. A year earlier Bedle had charged a largely Republican grand jury, empaneled by a Republican sheriff, to investigate the thirty-two aldermen so abused by the *Evening Journal*. Although three men who later became commissioners sat on that jury, one as foreman, they had returned no indictments against any of the aldermen. The men who heard Bedle's 1872 charge, however, returned 148 indictments against the seventeen commissioners and two police justices appointed by the legislature. Comprising men from all Hudson County, the grand jury's most prominent members came from Jersey City's Democratic elite. The foreman, Thomas Aldridge, had been Hudson City's recorder before consolidation, and Orestes Cleveland and John Van Vorst, both former mayors of Jersey City, also sat on the jury. Schoolmaster James Brann represented Irish "respectability." Although the jury would later be attacked as "packed" and "partisan," the New York Herald claimed that only eight were Democrats, with twelve Republicans and four independents.[10] Sitting for two months instead of the usual two weeks, this grand jury developed a unique consciousness which colored not only its indictments but its subsequent presentment.[11]

Although secret by law, the grand jury procedings appeared in the New York Herald, much to the distress of Judge Bedle, and even in the local Republican press. Probably written by Patrick O'Brien, active in the Young Democrats a year earlier, the Herald's articles told of excessive survey costs, non-competitive bidding on minor contracts, and commissioners buying property on streets to be improved.[12] Furious at the Herald's articles, Z. K. Pangborn filled the Journal with abuse of the "partisan" grand jury. One grand juror--a Republican--entered the *Journal* office with the intention of assaulting the absent Pangborn.[13] Sifting through the books of each commission, with strict literalness the grand jury compared official acts to what the city charter had prescribed. In late February they began to release their indictments.

Indicting every appointed official on one charge or another, they uncovered offenses that ranged from the serious to the trivial. They accused Bumsted, for example, of defrauding the city of thirty thousand dollars. They charged the police commissioners with assessing officers for political contributions and advancing them salary to pay the assessments. Two police justices allegedly retained fines for longer than twenty-four hours before turning them over to the city treasurer, a violation of the charter, and owned twenty-five dollars worth of stock each in the *Wacht am Hudson*, a German Republican paper that did business with the city. Returning a total of 148 indictments, the grand jury began a process of harassment and demoralization that would last as long as the commissions.[14]

Not content with merely indicting the commissioners, seventeen of the twenty-four grand jurors sent an open letter to both houses of the legislature demanding "relief from the fraudulent and burdensome charter foisted upon the city by a former Legislature." Reviewing the rising debt and the indictments already handed down, they found the flaw not in the character of those indicted but in the system that led to their indictment. "We are convinced," they wrote, "that the true remedy lies in a complete restoration of local government to the hands of the people interested." Democrat Henry Gaede read the grand jurors' letter in the Assembly, but when Senator John McPherson attempted to read it in the Senate, his colleagues prevented him, as it was "disrespectful" and insulting.[15]

Handed to the court two weeks later, the presentment reiterated this theme. "In the opinion of the Grand Jury," they wrote, "much of the evil complained of would disappear if the local government were restored to the people themselves." The administration of justice also received sharp rebuke. Two appointed police justices had replaced Recorder Martindale in 1871; both were native-born Protestants, one of New England background. Condemning their harsh punishments, the grand jury complained that they sentenced men "for long terms for very trivial offenses," not only burdening the state, but "depriving their families of support."[*] The presentment ended with an attack

---

[*] The police justices were not alone in supporting harsher punishments for minor offenses. The 1871 aldermen passed an ordinance prescribing ten days maximum imprisonment for violations of any city ordinance that previously carried no prison sentence. Vetoed by Mayor O'Neill as "very arbitrary and extraordinary," it never took effect. Manual of the Aldermen of Jersey City, 1871-1872 (Jersey City, 1872), p. 46.

on the city's press. Noting that these papers were "subsidized . . . by those whom we have been obliged . . . to indict . . . for diverse offenses," they criticized the "persistent attacks . . . upon this Inquest," which sought to bring "our deliberations into contempt and frustrate our sworn duty of bringing to justice all violators of the law."[16] Significantly, the grand jury demanded that the presentment be published not only in the county's official papers, but also in the New York Herald and New York Staats-Zeitung.[17]

Like the charter itself, the indictments received state-wide attention. Comparisons with Tammany, while hardly apt, appeared frequently.[18] Governor Joel Parker told a New York Herald reporter that "some of the best citizens" in Hudson County sat on the grand jury and that the publicity would result in either modification or repeal of the 1871 charter. Parker himself had blasted the commissions in his inaugural address in early 1872. "All honor to the noble Grand Jury," wrote O'Brien in the Herald.[19]

A week after the inquest ended, the first trial began. Choosing from a wealth of indictments, District Attorney Abram Q. Garretson and Attorney General Robert Gilchrist moved first against the police commissioners. The charge was fraud. Four police captains had received

a two hundred dollar advance in salary in the fall of
1871. Coincidentally, each then made a two hundred dollar contribution to campaign expenses. Although the commissioners claimed that this was a loan to tide the men
through the winter months and unrelated to the voluntary
contributions, no repayments had been made until after
the grand jury began its investigation.[20]

While the amount of money involved was not large,
the trial had great symbolic importance. If the commissioners lost, commission government was doomed in Jersey
City. Through the grand jury and the courts, the people
could effectively hamstring the commissioners. This point
was not lost on any one involved. The grand jury made it
plain in its presentment, and Pangborn showed his awareness by his vituperative attacks on the grand jury itself.
The commissioners knew the importance of this case too,
and sought to meet the challenge outside the court as well
as in. Looking to the legislature first, the commissioners introduced and lobbied for bills that would have established a county jury commission and also changed the
city charter to allow the business practices with regard
to contracts and bidding that had resulted in most indictments. Both bills failed.[21]

A second line of defense lay in jury manipulation.
The police commissioners secretly detailed officers to

mingle with the 148-member jury panel to ascertain their feelings. Revealed in court, this embarrassed all concerned and infuriated Judge Bedle. When finally selected, the jury was nearly a cross-section of Hudson County society, including a merchant, a builder, a clerk, three store-keepers, a saloon owner, a blacksmith, a seaman, and a bridge tender. Only six came from Jersey City, the rest from the small towns outside the city. In questioning prospective jurors, defense lawyers challenged all who read the New York Herald.[22]

Three of the city's ablest lawyers, Jonathan Dixon, Leon Abbett, and Charles H. Winfield, defended the commissioners. Only Dixon was a Republican. Basing their defense on the grounds that there was no intent to defraud, they also attempted to discredit the trial as a political witch hunt. Dixon referred to the jury as "the Tribunal" until rebuked from the bench; Abbett claimed he could not tell whether he was "in a State council, on a political rostrum, or in a court room; it would almost seem as if the jury was to register a verdict already found by the public."[23] Lasting six days, the courtroom always packed, the trial was followed by the New York papers as well as by the local press. The prosecution showed that the advances to the officers equalled their party contributions and that repayment began only after fraud was suspected; the commissioners were thus guilty of conspiracy to defraud the city. Putting all five commissioners on the stand, the defense claimed that the pay advances were only to help the men weather the winter on an inadequate salary of $1300. They were at a loss, however, to explain why the advances had not been deducted from later pay checks as they had purportedly agreed to do.[24] When Judge Bedle charged the jury, he told them that their verdict hinged on the commissioners' intent. If the money was a loan, then they were innocent. If the motive was to increase the officers' total annual salary above the charter-stipulated $1300, then they were guilty. Retiring at 4:45 p. m. on March 25, the jury brought in a verdict of guilty seventy-five minutes later.[25] Sentencing, Bedle decided, would await the conclusion of other cases during the court's next term.

Two months later the next case came to trial, a case involving public works commissioner Bumsted, a man often connected with official frauds in the past. Informed by Bumsted that the city planned to build a new reservoir on Bergen Hill, Garrett Vreeland, a real estate agent and Sunday School teacher from one of Bergen's oldest families, bought most of the land at the site for $153,710 and sold it to the city two months later for $189,470. Vreeland had borrowed $40,000 from Bumsted just prior to purchasing the land and repaid it just after receiving his money from the city. Bank deposit records also indicated that they had probably split the profits, about $30,000.[26] When Vreeland, on the witness stand, denied the charges, Judge Bedle gaveled down the laughter in the packed court room with great difficulty. As the evidence was circumstantial, defense lawyer Dixon argued that while his clients' behavior was indefensible, it demonstrated incompetence, not fraud.[27]

When Attorney General Gilchrist summed up for the state, he played on the relationship between the frauds and the idea of commission government itself, smearing the charter with the misdeeds of its servants:

> This conspiracy was so wicked, so detestable, that I could not exaggerate its character by the use of the strongest language. These men, clothed with great powers by the Legislature use those powers not for the protection of the property of the people but for purposes of tyranny and oppression which would not be tolerated in any other country in the world. If these things had been done in Berlin or Paris, or in any monarchical country, the throne would not be secure forty-eight hours. . . .
>
> Why, gentlemen, this is tyranny; this is oppression of the citizen, and invasion of the sacred rights of property, and when you interfere with this man's property, you interfere with my liberty. But thank God we have yet the jury box--. . . . This is really a question of your liberty and mine; it is a question of where we have to protect ourselves.[28]

Bedle reviewed the evidence in his charge to the jury and

virtually demanded conviction. "Gentlemen," he said, "you will do your duty (striking the bench with his clenched hand and knitting his brow) though it strikes hard." The jury took ten minutes to convict.[29]

Sentencing took place a week later. During that week Bumsted resigned as a commissioner, and the native-born elite, the same men who had sought to increase the police justices' power to imprison for petty violations, exerted great pressure to get Judge Bedle to be merciful. Standing before the court with tears in his eyes, his father (a founding member of the First Baptist Church) sobbing openly nearby, Bumsted heard his sentence: nine months at hard labor and a $500 fine. Bedle hoped that his sternness would "restrain others, so inclined, from immoral acts when entrusted with the interests of the people." Vreeland, home in bed in a nervous prostration, could not be sentenced until a week later. Here the court showed unexpected mercy. Noting that Vreeland did not commit his crimes as a public official, Bedle offered to impose only a fine if Vreeland refunded his profits to the city, a proposition quickly accepted by the convicted Sunday School teacher.[30] Other considerations may have played a role as well. "Mr. Vreeland is not an adventurer as Bumsted is," the New York Times noted, "but belongs to an old and honorable family. He is one of the wealthiest and has been one of the most highly respected citizens of Jersey City."[31] The immigrant "adventurer" went to jail; the "respected citizen" did not.

The court next turned its attention to sentencing the police commissioners, convicted two months before. Drawing the distinction between fraud for private and fraud for party gain, Bedle sentenced the five commissioners to a fine of one hundred dollars each. "Had you obtained this money for the purpose of private gain," Bedle told the convicted commissioners, "nothing would have saved you from the State Prison, because the Court mean, so far as they in the exercise of their duty can prevent it, that office shall not be prostituted for private gain." While the fine itself was a lenient punishment, it was accompanied by the loss of certain citizenship rights: the five commissioners could no longer vote or appear as witnesses in a court of record.[32]

The only commissioner sentenced to jail, Bumsted remained unrepentent and unconvinced that he had committed a real crime. Petitioning the Court of Pardons in July, he claimed the price paid for the land by the city was a fair price. "This is not now denied by judges of real estate," he wrote, "and therefore, even had I made something out of it, the city has not been defrauded."[33] Here was an insight into Gilded Age morality. Fraud, as defined by Bumsted, was not private profit from public office, but only too much profit from public office. Still supported by Pangborn and the _Journal_, Bumsted eventually received a pardon, but in a backhanded way. It took effect on the day his prison term expired, preserving his right to vote, but hardly clearing his name.[34]

Similarly, members of the native-born elite rallied to the defense of the police commissioners. Petitions were circulated for presentation to the Court of Pardons immediately after the sentences were passed. Among the signatories were Orestes Cleveland and John Van Vorst, both former Democratic mayors and both members of the grand jury that indicted the commissioners in the first place.[35] Respectable men might differ on the appropriate form of government for Jersey City, but they would rally to the defense of respectable men faced with loss of their citizenship. Turned down by the Court of Pardons, the police commissioners regained their privileges by a special act of the 1873 legislature.[36]

These trials had a great importance in Jersey City. They had the effect of deranging commission government, of forcing it on the defensive, of ending a bold, aggressive approach to putting the streets in good repair and the socially "deviant" poor in jail. After the police commissioners lost their citizenship, Governor Parker declared their offices vacant and appointed four Democrats (two native-born, one German, and one Irish) to fill the vacancies.[37] The old commissioners held on, however, and finally won an eight-month court battle that kept them in office. But the "reform" of the department suffered.[38] Fire Commissioner Tilden, under indictment for buying a horse without seeking competitive bids, abruptly quit his job with the Erie Railroad and disappeared.[39] The Board of Public Works voted in April 1872 that they would begin no new construction in the following year, "except in cases of absolute necessity, and then only with a concurrent vote of the Board of Aldermen." They also voted not to improve streets without first getting the approval of frontage owners. By binding themselves to seek popular approval, the Board went a long way to meeting public criticism. President Morillo H. Gillette, however, remained confused by the opposition. Commenting on Board actions, "he could say in the presence of all assembled and in the presence of God that nothing had been done by the Board, save that which was for the best interests of the public."[40]

Indictments and trials did not cease with those of 1872. The indicted public works commissioners came to trial in January 1873, for giving a sewer repair job to William Robinson in 1871, without seeking bids. Claiming that the work was of an emergency nature, the commissioners blamed Bumsted, then in prison, for any and all irregularities that may have occurred. Deadlocked, the jury voted to acquit the commissioners of defrauding the city, but to censure them for loose business practices. The verdict was a compromise, reached only after the jury had been locked in the jury room for twenty-two consecutive hours without food. The judge refused to accept the censure as part of the verdict; hence they were, in effect, acquitted.[41] Although no more cases were tried, every grand jury between 1873 and 1876 brought in more indictments against the state-appointed commissioners. Many were quashed for lack of evidence of intent to defraud; others remained as mute reminders of the power of the courts over the commissions. When commission government ended in 1877, the Jersey City Herald counted 115 indictments that had been neither killed nor tried. After 1873, however, there were no more trials.[42]

The panic of 1873 and the ensuing depression also left their mark on the financially over-extended city. Taxes, especially Board of Public Works assessments, went unpaid, and the city hovered close to bankruptcy until prosperity returned. Unable to sell its bonds or to collect its taxes, government came to a virtual stand-still.[43] Additionally, railroad expansion in the city took more property off the tax rolls, for railroads in New Jersey had been exempted from local taxation since 1830. Not surprisingly, the first sustained effort for equal railroad taxation in New Jersey began in Jersey City in 1873.[44]

The problems with and resistance to the 1871 commission charter led to a movement to change the government once more. Created in December 1871, the Citizens Association sought a modified charter that would create a government by the people and for the people but not exactly of the people. A number of men who had supported the 1871 charter now favored revision, and the reformers, members of the city's elite, came from both parties. Significantly, Fitzpatrick Democrats, representing the Irish elite, also joined in these deliberations.

Fitting the pattern of Gilded Age liberal reformers as described by John G. Sproat, these men knew more what they wanted to avoid than what they wanted to create.[45] They saw the commissions as too remote from the people, but at the same time would not countenance returning to aldermanic rule on the 1870 model. They sought "to purify public affairs" and "to rise above the corruption of political primaries." They wanted government without politics, especially partisan politics. Dr. Isaac N. Quimby, the President, described the association's purpose as "the welfare of the whole community, without any regard for party whatsoever." Stephen B. Ransom more explicitly expressed the reformers' reluctance to place party before principle. "He had never found one party more honest than another," the Jersey City Times reported him as saying; "a politician is a politician wherever you find him; he had been a Republican and a Democrat, and between both parties there was a remarkable similarity."[46]

Wrestling with governmental reform, they faced a dilemma: how to return power to the "people" without risking that it fall to the "wrong people." Reviewing the "corrupt" ward politics of 1870 in the Jersey City Times, "X" offered the Citizens Association some advice: "The people or citizens must offer inducements for another class to come forward and undertake management," he wrote. "They must devise a plan by which the better class can get control of the city government."[47] When an association member suggested merely abolishing the commissions, he received no support. Instead, the Times editorialized: "In view of the sense of relief that greeted the overthrow of the late Board of Aldermen, we think the people are scarcely prepared for this radical change."[48]

In a series of letters to the local press in January 1872 Jacob Weart, a Republican lawyer, presented a governmental schema which he hoped would solve the association's problems. Born in rural New Jersey in 1829, Weart had never held public office, although he had run for the assembly in 1856 and 1861. Then an abolitionist "of the Wendell Phillips school," Weart had also been active in local missionary work and was treasurer of the city's Congregational church. Although the author of the city's 1866 police commission bill, Weart had opposed Dixon's 1871 charter because of the lack of institutionalized restraint upon the public works commission.[49]

Weart began by setting the growth of urban government in its historical perspective:

> It is a well acknowledged and demonstrated fact that in this country we know how to govern our Nation and States, but do not know how to govern our cities. And the difficulty about our cities have been that they have sprung up from small villages, and governments established for villages have clung to the towns in their larger growth; and experience teaches us that a large city requires a different form of government; and but little united effort has been made as yet in this country to devise a suitable plan for the government of large cities raising and expending large sums of money.

In outlining a suitable plan, he distinguished between legislative and executive functions. A Common Council and mayor elected by the people should pass all laws and order all improvements. They would, in short, set policy. But no more. Policy would be executed by various departments--police, streets, water, education, etc.--each headed by an appointed official. While considering mayoral appointments adequate, Weart felt that gubernatorial appointment would be even more desirable. The appointment of the city's executives, he felt, had to be removed as far as possible from local politics. At the same time their compensation had to be adequate to support them as members of the social class from which Weart presumed they would come:

> In this plan the city must depart from the parsimony of having a large amount of time and the ablest and best talent in our midst to serve as a gratuity for the public good; the most honest and faithful men have the highest regard for their families and their own credit and maintenance, for it requires all the energies of honest hands to maintain families in these times; yet public clamor greatly censures many of our best men for not taking public positions in our city government, and finds great fault because the lower order of men get control.

As a middle class reformer, Weart associated public control by "the lower order of men" with venality without ever considering the truth of the proposition. "The reason is that the higher order of men cannot afford" public service, he wrote, "and the lower order come in with the aim and intent of making all they can."[50]

Five days later, in a second letter, Weart elaborated still further. The mayor and common council, attuned to the vagaries of taxpayers, would raise money. The appointed department heads would spend it in a professional and dispassionate manner.[51] Reviewing Weart's articles in the

Journal, Pangborn felt that to give the aldermen any power at all would restore the frightful situation that existed in 1870. Weart responded, not by exonerating the 1870 aldermen, but by claiming that in depriving the aldermen of the power to disperse funds, their power for harm was severely curtailed. The taxpayers had to be represented: "So said the men who fought the Revolution and established this nation."[52]

Endorsed by the Republican Times and the Democratic Standard, Weart's plan was almost immediately adopted by the Citizens Association as the basis for charter reform. His letters were read aloud at the meeting following their publication, and he formally joined the Association.[53] Transforming Weart's outline into a bill within a week, the Association appointed a committee to take it to Trenton and have it introduced into the legislature. The New York Herald saw Weart's plan as ideal. "The bill has some excellent features of a conservative character," the paper editorialized, "which would rescue the people of Jersey City from the ring thieves on the one hand and the bummers who stuff ballot boxes on the other."[54] That the 1870 aldermen had been "bummers" was an accepted truth by 1872 and rarely challenged.*

---

*A New York Herald reader, however, caught the irony of the 1871 "reform" charter. Signing himself "An American Democrat and a Jerseyman," he noted that every Jersey City

Although the Association's membership remains obscure, the composition of the committee to lobby in Trenton was indicative of divisions within the organization. Two native-born Protestants, one a vocal prohibitionist, and one Irish Catholic active in the Irish Emigrant Aid and Land Colonization Society went to Trenton.[55] This arrangement was not unusual. As the Association contained many former Young Democrats, most committees seem to have included one--and only one--Irish member. Never articulated, this procedure probably reflected the tensions within the society as native-born Protestants, a few of whom had been Know-Nothings, sat down with successful Irish Catholics to achieve a common end.[56]

The Citizens Association was not the only local group seeking charter revision. Meeting in Dudley S. Gregory's office, a dozen of the charter's original supporters convened to place limits on the authority of the Board of Public Works and Board of Finance and Taxation in order to meet the criticism without changing the basic commission structure. Known as the "taxpayers' amendments," these were also submitted to the legislature in the form of a

---

daily paper displayed "puritanical bigotry" toward "at least one-third of our citizen population." But only Bumsted, "an American and a Jerseyman," had gone to jail for defrauding the city. "Can the ring organ point to any such performance by an Irish Democrat in Jersey City?" he asked. "I guess not." (New York Herald, February 3, 1872.)

bill, with the approval of the Evening Journal.[57] A third bill, introduced by Hudson County Senator John McPherson, would have merely made the commissioners elective rather than appointive, a move which, claimed the Journal, would commit "the welfare of a great city to the tender mercies of a lot of Democratic gin mill caucuses."[58]

All this activity changed nothing. The state government killed all three bills. The Republican-controlled Senate defeated both McPherson's bill to make the commissioners' positions elective and Weart's charter to divide responsibility between commissioners and aldermen. Only the "taxpayers' amendments" passed, and Governor Parker vetoed them. Opposed to commissions on principle, Parker seems to have felt that these changes would have made ultimate repeal more difficult.[59]

Repeal of the commission did not come for another five years. From 1873 to 1875, different reform groups attempted to push the Weart charter or a variant through the legislature but without success. The Democratic Assembly and the Republican Senate could not agree on how to end commission government in Jersey City. In 1875 a legislative amendment that forbade special legislation made it impossible to pass legislation for a specific community. Two years later Leon Abbett, then Senator from Hudson County, cut through the constitutional requirement that all legislation be general in its effects. A simple measure, Abbett's bill merely made every commission appointed for a municipality elective. Although never mentioning Jersey City, this "general legislation" applied no where else.[60]

While elected commissioners replaced appointed commissioners in 1877, the basic structure designed by Jonathan Dixon in 1871 remained intact. The three commissions--police, fire, and public works--each now had six members, one from each of the six aldermanic districts, serving two-year staggered terms. Hardly a success with appointed officials, Dixon's charter was a disaster with elected men. With so many elected bodies, responsibility, instead of being concentrated, was so diffused as to render the government ineffective. Because the 1871 gerrymander remained, native-born Republicans were often able to elect three members to a board, deadlocking proceedings for months at a time.[61]

More importantly, after 1877 Jersey City again became a city with an immigrant government. Pangborn worried that after the appointed commissions departed, native-born citizens would be unable to hold office again. By 1885 the most influential politician in the city was Robert Davis, born in Ireland in 1848. Davis continued as leader of the local Democratic party until his death in 1911; Frank Hague quickly replaced him.[62] The assumption of political power by the city's Irish that had occurred between 1860 and 1870 continued after the interruption that lasted from 1871 to 1877.[63]

Native-born resistance to Irish influence had lasted a quarter of a century. Recognizing the threat in 1853, the Hudson County Bible Society had warned that unless measures were taken, the "foreign element which is so rapidly flowing into this country is destined, at no distant day, to exert an immense, if not controlling influence in our county affairs, both political and religious."[64] Through the 1850's native-born Protestants effectively controlled all aspects of the city's municipal institutions and manipulated them in consciously anti-Catholic ways. Feeling oppressed, the city's Irish worked first to control the processes of justice and then other aspects of governmental life. By 1870 Irish Democrats not only filled most elective offices, but challenged the native-born leadership directly. Uniting around shared nativistic views, native-born Republicans and Democrats reacted to artisan immigrant officeholders by literally abolishing local government in Jersey City. Rising debt, political trials, and the financial embarrassment caused by the depression discredited the legislative commissions. Only then did the city's government again come under popular control, and only then was the transfer of power so presciently foreseen by the Bible Society a quarter of a century before completed.

DOCUMENTATION: CHAPTER VIII

[1] *Jersey City Herald*, April 1, 1871.

[2] *New York Herald*, February 16, 1872; *New York Times*, January 19, 1873.

[3] *Standard*, November 7, 1871; McLean, pp. 84-88.

[4] "Jonathan Dixon tells the whole Republican party . . . that the people of Jersey City don't know how to govern themselves." *Standard*, November 7, 1871; *Jersey City Times*, November 6, 1871.

[5] *Irish World*, May 6, 1871.

[6] *Jersey City Times*, November 9, 1871.

[7] *Irish American*, November 4, 1871.

[8] *Jersey City Times*, December 11, 1871; January 23, 1872.

[9] *Ibid.*, January 15, 1872.

[10] *Journal*, January 16, 18, 31, 1871; *New York Herald*, February 8, 1872.

[11] *Journal*, January 15, 1872.

[12] *Ibid.*, January 31, 1872; *New York Herald*, February 3, 6, 16, 1872.

[13] See, for example, *Journal*, March 5, 6, 7, 1872; *Jersey City Times*, February 22, 1872.

[14] The indictments appeared in all the newspapers after February 22, 1872. The *Journal* provided a summary, March 13, 1872.

[15] *Jersey City Times*, February 29, March 1, 1872.

[16] *Ibid.*, March 12, 1872.

[17] *Journal*, March 11, 1872.

[18] *Trenton State Gazette* (n. d.), quoted in *Journal*, March 7, 1872; *New York Herald*, February 16, 1872.

[19] *New York Herald*, February 16, 17, 1872.

[20] Jersey City Times, March 19, 1872.

[21] New York Herald, March 5, 1872; New York Tribune, March 15, 1872.

[22] Journal, March 21, 1872.

[23] New York Times, March 26, 1872; New York Herald, March 27, 1872.

[24] Jersey City Times, March 23, 25, 1872.

[25] Ibid., March 26, 1872.

[26] New York Herald and New York Times, May 22, 1872.

[27] New York Herald, June 1, 1872.

[28] Ibid., June 2, 1872.

[29] Journal, June 3, 1872.

[30] New York Times, June 15, 1872.

[31] Ibid., June 3, 1872.

[32] New York Herald, June 23, 1872; Journal, June 24, 1872.

[33] Journal, July 29, 1872.

[34] Ibid., December 3, 1872.

[35] Ibid., June 24, 1872.

[36] New York Times, January 22, 1873; New York Herald, February 14, 1872.

[37] Journal, August 3, 1872. There were only four vacancies because one commissioner's term had expired and been filled by the legislature in March 1872.

[38] Ibid., July 8, 1872, through February 27, 1873, passim.

[39] Ibid., July 9, 1873.

[40] Jersey City Times, April 16, 1872.

[41] New York Herald, January 9, 10, 1872.

[42] Jersey City Herald, June 26, 1875; June 9, 1877.

43New York Herald, January 20, May 13, 1873; McLean, pp. 86, 91.

44Jacob Weart, Untaxed Corporation Property in Jersey City (Jersey City, 1873).

45John G. Sproat, "The Best Men:" Liberal Reformers in the Gilded Age (New York, 1968), pp. 46-69.

46Journal, January 5, 1872; Jersey City Times, January 12, 1872.

47Jersey City Times, January 11, 1872.

48Ibid., January 5, 1872.

49Standard, November 5, 1861; McLean, p. 214.

50Jersey City Times, January 6, 1872.

51Ibid., January 11, 1872.

52Ibid., January 12, 1872.

53Ibid., January 12, 1872. Weart's letters were also influential in the thinking of New York City's Committee of Seventy, an elite group attempting municipal reform in the wake of the Tweed Ring. Ibid., January 20, 27, 1872.

54New York Herald, March 27, 1872.

55Jersey City Times, January 19, 1872.

56Ibid.; Journal, February 2, 1872.

57Jersey City Times, January 17, 1872.

58Journal, March 27, 1872.

59Standard, April 4, 5, 1872; New York Herald, April 12, 1872.

60Jersey City Herald, April 14, 1877.

61The Board of Public Works that took office on May 1, 1882, for example, did not effect an organization until late July of that year. Truth (New York), July 25, 1882.

62New York Times, January 10, 1911; Richard J. Connors, "The Local Political Career of Mayor Frank Hague" (Ph. D. Dissertation, Columbia, 1966), pp. 10-20.

[63] In 1882, for example, the elected Hudson County Board of Freeholders, dominated by Jersey City members, resembled the 1870 Board of Aldermen in its ethnic complexion. Eight Irish-born or children of Irish-born, five native-born, two Germans, and a Welshman sat on the Board. Journal, January 13, 19, 1882.

[64] First Annual Report of the Hudson County Bible Society, 1853 (New York, 1853), p. 7.

A NOTE ON SOURCES

Jersey City's newspapers are the most important sources used in this dissertation. At least two daily papers, as well as a number of weeklies, are extant for the entire period, 1850-1877. Overshadowed by New York City, however, Jersey City never developed a full complement of ethnic or religious newspapers, nor did it have more than three dailies. Further, all of these papers were edited by and for native-born Protestants. The city they describe was middle-class, anti-immigrant, and anti-Catholic; nativism suffuses their approach to social questions. A look at the major papers and their editors clearly illustrates this point.

During the 1850's the city's two dailies were the Democratic <u>Telegraph</u> and the Whig <u>Sentinel</u>. Both were outspokenly anti-Catholic and anti-Irish, giving much space to the Know-Nothings. The weekly <u>Courier</u>, published in 1856 and 1857 by William Dunning, was more explicitly Know-Nothing but no more nativistic than its Democratic and Whig competitors. In 1858 Dunning bought the <u>Sentinel</u>, merged it with his <u>Courier</u>, and began a daily, the <u>Courier and Advertiser</u>. Joining the army in 1862, Dunning closed the paper, but returned to local journalism in 1867 when he helped found the <u>Evening Journal</u> with Zebina K. Pangborn.

The *Journal* maintained an anti-Irish and anti-Catholic stance throughout the nineteenth century.

The *Telegraph* ceased publication in 1859, and the facilities were soon bought by John Lyons, a former state O. U. A. officer seeking to revive the American party. Published as the *American Standard*, the paper became Democratic by 1861, but maintained the nativistic views of its publisher until sold to a second-generation Irishman in 1875. Before 1875, the city had no daily newspaper not identified with anti-Catholicism and nativism. The news of the immigrant communities was ignored, and the Irish received attention mostly as paupers, criminals, and drunkards.

New York City newspapers circulated in Jersey City, but their coverage of New Jersey news was haphazard at best. New York's Irish papers, nonetheless, proved invaluable in studying the Jersey City Irish community. While their coverage of Jersey City was hardly comprehensive, they were at least award of the existence of Irish nationalist societies, Catholic temperance organizations, etc. Of the New York dailies, the *New York Herald* was the most useful, especially during the early 1870's, when Patrick O'Brien, an articulate Irishman, wrote lengthy accounts of Jersey City politics, the only accounts found that gave attention to explicitly Irish views.

Two local histories were published in the late nineteenth century. William H. Shaw published his *History of Essex and Hudson Counties, New Jersey*, in 1884. Dwelling primarily on the colonial period, Shaw showed little interest in the nineteenth century immigrant city. More comprehensive is Alexander McLean's *History of Jersey City, N. J.*, published in 1894. An *Evening Journal* reporter for almost two decades, McLean was both observer and participant in the conflicts between native-born and immigrants. Although quite useful, the volume is permeated with a sense of regret that the forces of Evil had gradually conquered the forces of Good in Jersey City. Both books provide good biographical information on elite political leaders and businessmen.

Few secondary sources relate directly to this study; New Jersey in the nineteenth century has not been a subject favored by historians. Yet as a state that became one of the most heavily urbanized and industrialized in the nation, it should provide useful clues as to how these processes worked in nineteenth century America. Mayor Kenneth Gibson of Newark has said that wherever American cities are going, Newark will get there first. Where American cities go will be determined in part by where they have been.

BIBLIOGRAPHY

Jersey City Newspapers

American Standard. 1859-1875.

Argus. 1875-1877.

Daily Sentinel and Advertiser. 1848-1862.

Daily Telegraph. 1854-1858.

Evening Journal. 1867-1882, 1891, 1896.

Hudson County Courier. 1856-1857.

Jersey City Chronicle. 1863-1864.

Jersey City Gazette. 1870-1871.

Jersey City Herald. 1870-1871, 1873-1887.

Jersey City News. 1896.

Jersey City Times. 1865-1873.

Other Newspapers

Hudson County Democrat (Hoboken). 1864-1867.

Irish American (New York). 1868-1880.

Irish World (New York). 1870-1882.

Newark Daily Advertiser. 1859, 1866, 1870-1871.

New York Freeman's Journal and Catholic Register. 1866-1868, 1874.

New York Herald. 1859, 1870-1873, 1875-1876.

New York Sun. 1867-1871.

New York Times. 1853-1877.

New York Tribune. 1859-1872.

Truth (New York). 1882.

World (New York). 1861-1866.

Other Primary Sources

American Tract Society. *General Views of Colporteurage* (n.p., n.d.).

Charter of Jersey City and Supplements (Jersey City, 1873).

First Annual Report of the Hudson County Bible Society, 1853 (New York, 1853).

Fourth Annual Report of the Hudson County Bible Society, 1856 (Jersey City, 1857).

Home Evangelization: A View of the Wants and Prospects of the Country Based on the Facts and Relations of Colportage (n.p., n.d.).

Manuals of the Board of Aldermen of Jersey City. 1857-1875.

Reports of the President and Superintendent of the New York and Erie Railroad for the Year Ending September 30, 1855 (New York, 1855).

Robson, Charles (ed.). *The Biographical Encyclopedia of New Jersey in the Nineteenth Century* (Philadelphia, 1877).

State of New Jersey, Department of State, Census Bureau. *Compendium of Censuses, 1726-1905, Together with the Tabulated Returns of 1905* (Trenton, 1906).

A Statement of the Operation of the New York and Erie Railroad Under the Receivership from August 16, 1859, to December 31, 1861 (New York, 1862).

United States Census (1860, 1870, 1880). Schedule of Manufactures, Jersey City, New Jersey (Manuscript, New Jersey State Library, Trenton, New Jersey).

United States Census (1860). Schedule of Population, Jersey City, New Jersey (National Archives Microfilm Publication, Roll 653-693).

Verrinder, William. *Report of the City Missionary to the Board of Managers of the Hudson County Bible Society* (Jersey City, 1857).

Weart, Jacob. *Untaxed Corporation Property in Jersey City* (Jersey City, 1873).

Secondary Sources

Billington, Ray Allen. *The Protestant Crusade 1800-1860* (Quadrangle ed., Chicago, 1964).

Bland, Sister Joan. *The Story of the Catholic Total Abstinence Union of America* (Lancaster, 1951).

Bogart, Ernest L. *Peacham: The Story of a Vermont Hill Town* (Montpelier, 1948).

Connors, Richard J. "The Local Political Career of Mayor Frank Hague" (Ph.D. dissertation, Columbia University, 1966).

Costello, Augustine E. *History of the Police Department of Jersey City* (Jersey City, 1891).

Curran, Thomas J. "The Know Nothings in New York" (Ph.D. dissertation, Columbia University, 1963).

Fitzpatrick, William J. *The Life of the Very Rev. Thomas N. Burke, O.P.* (London, 1894).

Formisano, Ronald P. *The Birth of Mass Political Parties Michigan, 1827-1861* (Princeton, 1971).

Gibbs, Joseph C. *History of the Catholic Total Abstinence Union* (Philadelphia, 1907).

Gough, John Francis. *St. Mary's in Jersey City: A History of the Parish* (New York, 1938).

Harrison, Brian H. *Drink and the Victorians: The Temperance Question in England, 1815-1872* (Pittsburgh, 1971).

Hays, Samuel P. "The Politics of Reform in Municipal Government in the Progressive Era," *Pacific Northwest Quarterly*, LV, No. 4 (October, 1964), pp. 157-169.

Higham, John. *Strangers in the Land: Patterns of Nativism, 1860-1925* (Atheneum ed., New York, 1963).

Hogarty, Richard A. "Leon Abbett of New Jersey: Precursor of the Modern Governor" (Ph. D. dissertation, Princeton, 1966).

Holt, Michael F. *Forging a Majority: The Formation of the Republican Party in Pittsburgh, 1848-1860* (New Haven, 1969).

Imbrie, Rev. Charles K. *History of the First Presbyterian Church of Jersey City, New Jersey* (New York, 1888).

Knapp, Charles M. *New Jersey Politics During the Civil War and Reconstruction* (Geneva, 1924).

Lane, Roger. *Policing the City: Boston, 1822-1885* (Cambridge, 1967).

Lipset, Seymour M. and Raab, Earl. *The Politics of Unreason: Right Wing Extremism in America, 1790-1970* (New York, 1970).

McLean, Alexander. *History of Jersey City, N. J.* (Jersey City, 1894).

Parnet, Robert D. "The Know Nothings in Connecticut" (Ph. D. dissertation, Columbia University, 1966).

Pessen, Edward. "The Egalitarian Myth and the American Social Reality: Wealth, Mobility, and Equality in the 'Era of the Common Man,'" *American Historical Review*, Vol. LXXVI, No. 4 (October, 1971).

Richardson, James F. *The New York Police: Colonial Times to 1901* (New York, 1970).

Rosenberg, Carroll S. *Religion and the Rise of the American City: The New York City Mission Movement, 1812-1870* (Ithaca, 1971).

Sackett, William E. *Modern Battles of Trenton.* 2 Vols. (Trenton, 1895; New York, 1914).

Shannon, William V. *The American Irish* (New York, 1963).

Shaw, William H. *History of Essex and Hudson Counties, New Jersey.* 2 Vols. (Philadelphia, 1884).

Shea, John G. *A History of the Catholic Church within the Limits of the United States.* 4 Vols. (New York, 1892).

Soule, Leon C. *The Know Nothing Party in New Orleans: A Reappraisal* (Baton Rouge, 1961).

Sproat, John G. *"The Best Men:" Liberal Reformers in the Gilded Age* (New York, 1968).

Thernstrom, Stephan. *Poverty and Progress: Social Mobility in a Nineteenth Century City* (Atheneum ed., New York, 1969).

Van Deusen, Glyndon. *Horace Greeley: Nineteenth Century Crusader* (New York, 1953).

Winfield, Charles H. *History of the County of Hudson, New Jersey* (New York, 1874).

Yeager, Sister M. Hildegarde. *The Life of James Roosevelt Bayley, First Bishop of Newark and Eighth Archbishop of Baltimore, 1814-1877* (Washington, 1947).

THE IRISH-AMERICANS

An Arno Press Collection

Athearn, Robert G. **THOMAS FRANCIS MEAGHER:** An Irish Revolutionary in America. 1949

Biever, Bruce Francis. **RELIGION, CULTURE AND VALUES:** A Cross-Cultural Analysis of Motivational Factors in Native Irish and American Irish Catholicism. 1976

Bolger, Stephen Garrett. **THE IRISH CHARACTER IN AMERICAN FICTION, 1830-1860.** 1976

Browne, Henry J. **THE CATHOLIC CHURCH AND THE KNIGHTS OF LABOR.** 1949

Buckley, John Patrick. **THE NEW YORK IRISH:** Their View of American Foreign Policy, 1914-1921. 1976

Cochran, Alice Lida. **THE SAGA OF AN IRISH IMMIGRANT FAMILY:** The Descendants of John Mullanphy. 1976

Corbett, James J. **THE ROAR OF THE CROWD.** 1925

Cronin, Harry C. **EUGENE O'NEILL:** Irish and American; A Study in Cultural Context. 1976

Cuddy, Joseph Edward. **IRISH-AMERICAN AND NATIONAL ISOLATIONISM, 1914-1920.** 1976

Curley, James Michael. **I'D DO IT AGAIN:** A Record of All My Uproarious Years. 1957

Deasy, Mary. **THE HOUR OF SPRING.** 1948

Dinneen, Joseph. **WARD EIGHT.** 1936

Doyle, David Noel. **IRISH-AMERICANS, NATIVE RIGHTS AND NATIONAL EMPIRES:** The Structure, Divisions and Attitudes of the Catholic Minority in the Decade of Expansion, 1890-1901. 1976

Dunphy, Jack. **JOHN FURY.** 1946

Fanning, Charles, ed. **MR. DOOLEY AND THE CHICAGO IRISH:** An Anthology. 1976

Farrell, James T. **FATHER AND SON.** 1940

Fleming, Thomas J. **ALL GOOD MEN.** 1961

Funchion, Michael F. **CHICAGO'S IRISH NATIONALISTS, 1881-1890.** 1976

Gudelunas, William A., Jr. and William G. Shade. **BEFORE THE MOLLY MAGUIRES:** The Emergence of the Ethno-Religious Factor in the Politics of the Lower Anthracite Region, 1844-1872. 1976

Henderson, Thomas McLean. **TAMMANY HALL AND THE NEW IMMIGRANTS:** The Progressive Years. 1976

Hueston, Robert Francis. **THE CATHOLIC PRESS AND NATIVISM, 1840-1860.** 1976

Joyce, William Leonard. **EDITORS AND ETHNICITY:** A History of the Irish-American Press, 1848-1883. 1976

Larkin, Emmet. **THE HISTORICAL DIMENSIONS OF IRISH CATHOLICISM.** 1976

Lockhart, Audrey. **SOME ASPECTS OF EMIGRATION FROM IRELAND TO THE NORTH AMERICAN COLONIES BETWEEN 1660-1775.** 1976

Maguire, Edward J., ed. **REVEREND JOHN O'HANLON'S *THE IRISH EMIGRANT'S GUIDE FOR THE UNITED STATES*:** A Critical Edition with Introduction and Commentary. 1976

McCaffrey, Lawrence J., ed. **IRISH NATIONALISM AND THE AMERICAN CONTRIBUTION.** 1976

McDonald, Grace. **HISTORY OF THE IRISH IN WISCONSIN IN THE NINETEENTH CENTURY.** 1954

McManamin, Francis G. **THE AMERICAN YEARS OF JOHN BOYLE O'REILLY, 1870-1890.** 1976

McSorley, Edward. **OUR OWN KIND.** 1946

Moynihan, James H. **THE LIFE OF ARCHBISHOP JOHN IRELAND.** 1953

Niehaus, Earl F. **THE IRISH IN NEW ORLEANS, 1800-1860.** 1965

O'Grady, Joseph Patrick. **IRISH-AMERICANS AND ANGLO-AMERICAN RELATIONS, 1880-1888.** 1976

Rodechko, James Paul. **PATRICK FORD AND HIS SEARCH FOR AMERICA:** A Case Study of Irish-American Journalism, 1870-1913. 1976

Roney, Frank. **IRISH REBEL AND CALIFORNIA LABOR LEADER:** An Autobiography. Edited by Ira B. Cross. 1931

Roohan, James Edmund. **AMERICAN CATHOLICS AND THE SOCIAL QUESTION, 1865-1900.** 1976

Shannon, James. **CATHOLIC COLONIZATION ON THE WESTERN FRONTIER.** 1957

Shaw, Douglas V. **THE MAKING OF AN IMMIGRANT CITY:** Ethnic and Cultural Conflict in Jersey City, New Jersey, 1850-1877. 1976

Sylvester, Harry. **MOON GAFFNEY.** 1947

Tarpey, Marie Veronica. **THE ROLE OF JOSEPH McGARRITY IN THE STRUGGLE FOR IRISH INDEPENDENCE.** 1976

Vinyard, JoEllen McNergney. **THE IRISH ON THE URBAN FRONTIER:** Nineteenth Century Detroit. 1976

Walsh, James P., ed. **THE IRISH: AMERICA'S POLITICAL CLASS.** 1976

Weisz, Howard Ralph. **IRISH-AMERICAN AND ITALIAN-AMERICAN EDUCATIONAL VIEWS AND ACTIVITIES, 1870-1900:** A Comparison. 1976